Evaluating
the Economics
of Complementary
and <u>Integrative Medicine</u>

PATRICIA M. HERMAN, ND, PHD

Foreword by Michael F. Drummond, PhD

Samueli Institute was a non-profit research organization investigating the safety, effectiveness and integration of healing-oriented practices and environments. They convened and supported expert teams to conduct research on natural products; nutrition and lifestyle; mind-body practices; and complementary and traditional approaches such as acupuncture, manipulation, yoga and the placebo (meaning) effect. They supported a knowledge network that assisted in integrating evidence-based information about healing into mainstream health care and community settings and in creating optimal healing environments.

This work was supported by the US Army Medical Research and Materiel Command under Award No.W81XWH-06-1-0279. The views, opinions and/or findings contained in this report are those of the author(s) and should not be construed as an official Department of the Army position, policy or decision unless so designated by other documentation.

Written by Patricia Herman.
Graphic Design by Six Half Dozen.
Formatting and republishing by CJ Rhoads.

This book was written by Dr. Herman while she was a Research Scientist in the Health Outcomes and PharmacoEconomic Research Center, College of Pharmacy, University of Arizona. She is presently a Senior Behavioral Scientist in the Health Division of RAND Corporation.

ISBN-13: 978-1-61305-015-6

CONTENTS

FOREWORD

In these tough financial times, it is no longer enough to demonstrate that a new therapy confers benefits. It is also necessary to show that the benefits justify the costs; that is, the value of the resources consumed. Therefore, it is important that practitioners in all fields become knowledgeable about the methods of *economic evaluation*, a family of techniques for comparing the costs and consequences of alternative treatments and programs.

The aim of this Handbook is to provide the reader with sufficient knowledge to understand and interpret published economic evaluations of healthcare options in general and of complementary and integrative medicine (CIM) in particular. A subsidiary aim is to give a good grounding in the basics for those interested in performing an economic evaluation, although it recommends that such individuals also seek the help of a health economist or other professional with experience in performing such studies.

The Handbook contains descriptions of all the basic methods of economic evaluation, presented in an accessible manner, along with plenty of examples. However, for me the most interesting aspect is the discussion of the particular challenges in attempting to conduct economic evaluations of CIM. These include challenges in the specification of the alternatives being evaluated, particularly when integrative clinics are being compared with more conventional service configurations, and in the assessment of outcomes.

One limitation of many economic evaluations of health care treatments and programs is that the favoured measure of benefit, the quality-adjusted life-year (QALY), may not capture all the relevant dimensions of patient benefit. In the case of CIM these can include benefits derived from the process of care, or those relating to the self-empowerment patients achieve through actively improving their health.

Another critical aspect of CIM is that a broad perspective on cost is required, because many costs fall outside the healthcare system, including costs borne by the patient. This raises both conceptual and measurement difficulties for economic evaluations in this field.

Nevertheless, as the Handbook rightly points out, new approaches for the measurement of costs and benefits should be pursued, as far as possible, within the standard rubric of economic evaluation, since ultimately those allocating scarce resources may need to make choices between investing in CIM, as compared to other fields of health care.

An important audience for this Handbook are those researchers conducting clinical evaluations of treatments or services in CIM. Economic evaluation relies on accurate and unbiased estimates of the effectiveness of therapies, typically obtained from controlled clinical trials. These can sometimes be a useful vehicle for economic data capture and clinical researchers should actively consider this option.

In the US, with the advent of comparative effectiveness research and the establishment of the Patient-Centered Outcomes Research Institute (PCORI), this is an opportune time to rethink the research agenda and to increase the emphasis on the assessment of benefits to patients.

This Handbook is very timely and should appeal to a wide audience in the field of complementary and integrative medicine.

Michael F. Drummond, PhD
July 12, 2012
Professor of Health Economics,
University of York,
York, UK.

CHAPTER 1. INTRODUCTION

Why should we care about the economics of complementary and integrative medicine (CIM)? Healthcare in the US is expensive and becoming more so every year. Policy and decision makers increasingly need information on costs, as well as effectiveness and safety, in order to formulate healthcare strategies that are both clinically effective and financially responsible. If CIM is to be considered in these strategies, its economic impact must be determined.

It is obvious that many people believe the benefits of CIM exceed its costs. Various surveys have shown that a substantial portion of the US population uses CIM and pays directly for that use.[1-4] The most recent estimates show that total US out-of-pocket expenditures for CIM were $34 billion—an amount that constitutes 11% of all US out-of-pocket healthcare expenditures.[1]

Theoretically, CIM seems a good candidate for cost-effectiveness, and even cost savings, because it avoids high technology, offers inexpensive and non-invasive remedies, encourages healthy lifestyle change, and focuses on the whole person, which may improve health beyond the targeted disease or condition. However, to many in the conventional healthcare system, CIM is seen only as an "add on" expense. What must be demonstrated via economic evaluation are the healthcare costs that can be avoided through the use of CIM.

CIM offers the potential for several avenues of cost reduction. The first is as a direct replacement for the usual conventional therapy for a condition. The second is in terms of lower future healthcare utilization both in general (through treating the whole person) and for the targeted disease or condition. A third avenue to cost reduction is through reducing productivity loss for employers. A reduction in costs to employers does not directly reduce healthcare costs (unless the employer is itself a healthcare facility); however, both are costs to society. Productivity losses can be reduced through improved employee health, and potentially through the improved employee well-being and empowerment offered by CIM.

Economic evaluation of complementary and integrative medicine

The concepts and techniques described in this handbook for the economic evaluation of CIM are the same as those used for conventional medicine.[5] This is necessary in order for results to be accepted and understood by the policy and decision makers who make decisions about, and allocate resources to, the various components of the healthcare system. However, there are some differences in how the techniques may be applied for CIM. Many of these differences were delineated by the Economic Toolkit Expert Panel Conference sponsored by the Samueli Institute and held January 2011 at the RAND Corporation offices in Santa Monica, CA. Below is a summary of the key aspects of economic evaluation particularly salient to CIM.

Patient perspective

Because much of CIM is accessed directly through patient self-referral and paid out-of-pocket, the patient's perception of whether the benefits of care exceed its cost is important. Thus, the practices and outcomes valued by the patient become critical in CIM. The patient perspective is, for the most part, ignored in economic evaluations of conventional medicine. It should be noted that the benefits of care to the patient may extend beyond health improvement for the condition of interest, and beyond health improvement in general. Patients may also derive value from the process of care (e.g., their relationship with their practitioner), or through the self-empowerment achieved through actively improving their health. These additional patient benefits can be missed if the context and goals of CIM and the patient perspective are not considered. The patient perspective is included in the discussion of the third principle in Chapter 2, and the additional non-health benefits seen by patients are discussed in Chapter 6.

Availability of data on the effectiveness of therapies

Economic evaluation requires information on both the health benefits (i.e., effectiveness) and costs of the therapies under consideration. There are many challenges involved in determining the effectiveness of CIM. By extension, these same challenges also affect economic evaluations of CIM. This is discussed in more detail in Chapter 6.

Appropriate and well-defined comparators

To be useful to healthcare policy and decision makers, the CIM therapy under consideration should be compared to some version of the care presently provided to that patient population (i.e., usual care). For generalizability and treatment fidelity, both need to be well-defined. One challenge in evaluating CIM is that it can be anything from a simple therapy (e.g., taking capsules containing the herb Willow bark) to multi-component collaborative care at an integrative medicine clinic. In an economic evaluation both comparators need to be defined to the level where their differences end. For example, comparing the use of Willow bark to an NSAID may only require a description of the contents of each capsule if both are administered by the same practitioner in the same clinic. Comparing care at an integrative clinic to care at a conventional clinic will require defining at least the different therapies offered, the types of practitioners involved and their training, the clinic setting, and any differences in how patients access each clinic. This is discussed in more detail when addressing the first principle in Chapter 2 and in Chapter 4.

Health outcomes and quality-adjusted life-years (QALYs)

Because CIM tends to address the whole person rather than target a specific symptom or disease, it can have a broader range of health impacts. Therefore, it is important to measure both a wide range of outcomes, and to consider using a summary measure of overall health that could capture the full range such as quality-adjusted life-years (QALYs). Care must be taken to use measures that are sensitive within the range of wellness seen in the target population. These issues are discussed in more detail in Chapter 6.

Measuring the costs of CIM

There are several systemic issues specific to CIM when measuring costs. These include the fact that since much of CIM is not covered by insurance, claims data are not readily available for analysis; that there is little published information on the cost or amount charged for individual CIM services; and since CIM can have broad health impacts, one must consider whether to capture all healthcare costs or only those related to the condition of interest. These are all discussed in Chapter 5.

What economic evaluation does and does not do

Economic evaluation adds information on costs to the information already available on a therapy's safety and effectiveness. Cost data are essential to allow for efficient resource allocation—i.e., to allow decision makers to identify the distribution of resources (funds, staff, equipment and facilities across various populations) that generates the greatest overall good. Because the results of economic evaluation bring this additional crucial information to a decision, there is sometimes the illusion that the results are "the answer." However, there are many considerations that go into a decision that are beyond the scope of an economic evaluation. For example, economic evaluations focus on efficiency—achieving the greatest total health gain possible from the resources available. They do not directly address equity—whether the costs and health gains are distributed fairly. They also do not address whether the therapies are legal, ethical, or politically acceptable. Therefore, although the results of economic evaluations can bring more information to a decision, they alone are not sufficient to make the decision.

A second main point is that although health outcomes are, to some extent, considered generalizable across settings, economic outcomes usually are not.[6] This is likely because human physiology and psychology tend to be more consistent and replicable across locations and settings than are resource availability, practice patterns and relative prices. Therefore, whereas meta-analysis can be used across the results of a number of trials to generate broad (i.e., generalizable) statements regarding the efficacy (or effectiveness) of a particular therapy for a particular health condition, similar broad statements regarding cost-effectiveness are usually not possible. In the face of this specificity regarding setting, one goal in economic evaluation is to ensure the *transferability* of study results—i.e., to provide enough study detail so that results can be adapted (usually via modeling) to other settings.[7] This will be discussed in more detail in Chapter 8.

How to use this handbook

The purpose of this handbook is to provide an introduction to the economic evaluation of healthcare options, with a specific emphasis on the economic evaluation of CIM. Attempts were made to strike a balance between providing knowledge sufficient for understanding and interpreting the results of economic evaluation, and the detail needed to perform an economic evaluation. The contents of this handbook should provide more than enough information to understand and interpret published economic evaluations of healthcare options in general, and of CIM in particular. Readers interested in performing an economic evaluation will receive a good grounding in the basics through this handbook, but will likely need to obtain and read many of the documents cited in order to acquire the detail needed for the full job. For those facing their first or a complicated economic evaluation, it is recommended that early in the planning process you obtain the services of a health economist or another professional with extensive experience performing these evaluations to ensure that your study generates the most valid, useful, and transferable results possible.

The next chapter gives four basic principles of economic evaluation. This information is crucial if you are new to the topic or have been away from economic evaluations for a while. The third chapter covers the concept of cost—the defining element of an economic evaluation. Economists, accountants, and lay persons each tend to have a different concept of cost. What is needed in an economic evaluation is the economists' version. Chapter 4 looks at the various ways one can perform an economic evaluation: alongside a clinical trial; using observational (e.g., medical chart or claims) data; and through decision analytic modeling, which uses existing or published data. Chapters 5 and 6 cover the measurement of health outcomes and of costs. The health outcomes chapter provides information on choosing the health effects to measure. Chapter 7 covers some of the analytical methods specific to economic evaluation. The final chapter discusses the interpretation and reporting of study results.

Terminology

The resources section contains reference to a complete guide for economic evaluation terminology. However, general definitions of some basic terms are introduced here to aid in understanding the concepts put forth by this handbook.

Benefits/Effects. Economic evaluations of healthcare options compare costs to health benefits. The health impacts of each option under consideration are often measured in effectiveness trials, and one type of economic evaluation (cost-benefit analysis) uses the monetary value of the health impact as the benefit. Therefore, where it is important to indicate that the topic is something other than cost-benefit analysis, the term "effect" rather than "benefit" will be used to refer to the health impact of an option.

Complementary/alternative/integrative medicine. The National Center for Complementary and Alternative Medicine (NCCAM) defines complementary and alternative medicine (CAM) "as a group of diverse medical and health care systems, practices, and products that are not generally considered part of conventional medicine."[8] NCCAM goes on to then define complementary medicine as the "use of CAM **together with** conventional medicine," and alternative medicine as the "use of CAM **in place of** conventional medicine."[8] In other words, complementary medicine is considered to be an "add-on" and alternative medicine a "substitute for" conventional care. However, in practice this distinction is less evident—essentially all CAM users take advantage of at least some conventional care,[3] and the use of CAM tends to substitute for some present and/or future conventional care.[9,10] Therefore, this handbook will use the term complementary and integrative medicine (CIM) to acknowledge both this lack of distinction and the emergence of integrative medicine, which, according to NCCAM, "combines treatments from conventional medicine and CAM for which there is some high-quality evidence of safety and effectiveness."[8]

Cost/Resource use/Unit cost/Opportunity cost/Savings. In economic evaluation, the term "cost" can have a different meaning than it does in general use (see Chapter 3 for more details). Although it is common to think of a cost as having a monetary value (e.g., something costs $X), it is actually the loss of resources used in making that thing that are its true cost. These resources are "used up" and no longer available for other purposes. The resources used are valued by multiplying the amount of each type of resource by its unit cost. The unit cost of each resource is its opportunity cost (i.e., how much that resource would have been worth if it had been used for its next best use). Although the term "cost" is most often thought of as a financial outlay, in an economic evaluation the term can represent either a positive or negative value—i.e., resource use can be increased or decreased. Often, the term cost savings will be used for a cost with a negative value.

Decision maker. A decision maker is any person or organization which makes (or influences) decisions regarding how much and which types of healthcare are made available or used. Decision makers can include government officials, executives of health insurance companies, medical directors of hospitals or clinics, physicians, patients, and patient caregivers. Decision maker, as it is used here, is a more specific term than stakeholder. A stakeholder is anyone who affects or is affected by a course of action, and a decision maker is specifically one who affects a course of action. To be most useful, economic evaluations are designed to provide needed, relevant information to a particular decision maker, type of decision maker, or set of decision makers. Different decision makers may value different outcomes and face different costs. Thus, the identity of the decision maker determines what is relevant and important to include in an economic evaluation.

Economic evaluation. The term economic evaluation generally refers to any study which includes the determination of the cost of something. A full economic evaluation involves the comparison of two or more alternatives in terms of both costs and effects. There are several types of full economic evaluation including cost-effectiveness analysis (CEA), cost-benefit analysis (CBA), and cost-utility analysis (CUA). In addition to these more commonly known approaches, a method will be described (see Chapter 2) which is especially important for reporting the results of an economic evaluation of CIM: cost consequence analysis (CCA). The general term "economic evaluation" will be used when not discussing a specific type.

Therapy/Comparators. Since economic evaluation is the comparison of two or more alternatives in terms of both costs and effects, the alternatives must be defined. In this handbook, the discussion focuses on the comparison of some form of CIM (or CIM plus usual care) to whatever is otherwise considered to be usual care (i.e., what is in place now). The CIM alternative under consideration may be a specific therapy such as an herb or nutritional supplement, a modality such as acupuncture or spinal manipulation, a discipline such as the use of a massage therapist or chiropractor, a whole medical system such as naturopathic medicine or homeopathy, or some other CIM model of care such as a multi-modality integrative medicine clinic. For simplicity, in this text the terms "therapy" or "intervention" will generally be used to represent any and all these options.

Chapter 2. Basic Principles of Economic Evaluation

Whether you are planning your own economic evaluation or are reading an economic evaluation from the literature, there are four main principles which will help you understand the basics of the analysis.

First principle: economic evaluation as a decision-making tool

Economic evaluation is performed to provide information which is useful to decision makers who are facing options—e.g., whether a new therapy should be offered or new approach to care adopted. The use of economic evaluation as a decision-making tool has at least three implications.

An added dimension of information. Because most decision makers desire safe and effective healthcare, they gain useful information from the results of clinical trials which indicate whether one therapy or approach is safe and more effective (e.g., better at reducing blood pressure) than another. Economic evaluation expands upon this by providing concurrent information on both effectiveness and cost. The added dimension of cost is important because few decision makers can ignore the cost implications of their choices. Adding costs to the analysis allows for the consideration of both effectiveness (i.e., whether something provides more health benefits) and efficiency (i.e., whether the additional effectiveness is worth the cost) in decisions.

Consider Figure 1. This is the type of information available to decision makers from effectiveness studies. This graph shows the results of four hypothetical effectiveness trials. Each of four new therapies (therapies A, B, C, and D) was compared to the therapy in current use (i.e., usual care). The height of the bar in each case indicates the amount that each therapy improves health over what it would have been under usual care. If you were a decision maker, which would you choose?

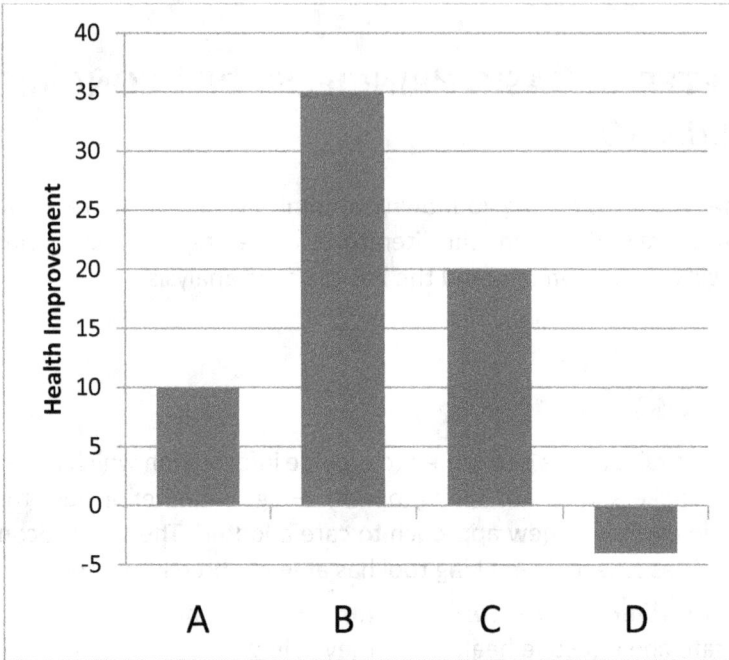

Figure 1. Effectiveness results for four therapies.

Most people would choose therapy B because it is the most effective—offers the largest health improvement. However, what if you also had the information available in **Figure** 2? What would your decision be now? In addition to considering effectiveness (i.e., options that will improve health) you would now have the ability to consider your budget and whether the additional health improvement was worth its cost. If your budget is tight, and you could take the savings and use them to do greater good in some other disease area, you may now choose therapy A, which offers both a health improvement and a cost savings of $100 per patient. On the other hand, if you had some money available in your budget and the additional health benefits were worth at least $4 per unit ($80/20 additional units of health improvement), you may now choose therapy C. Note that only in the case where you had the funds available and where these health improvements were worth at least $30 per unit ($1050/35) would you choose therapy B, even though it is the most effective.

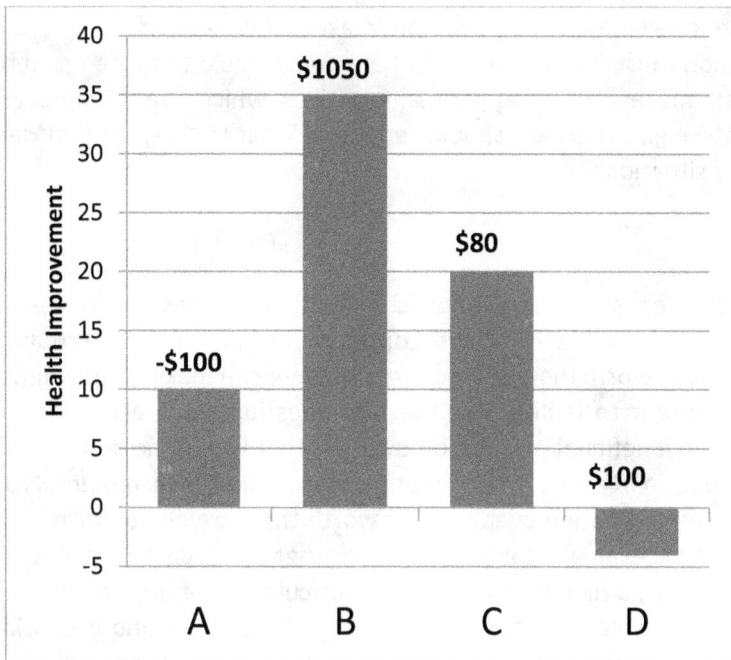

Figure 2. Effectiveness and cost results for four therapies.

Realistic comparisons. To be useful for decision makers, an economic evaluation has to compare costs and effectiveness between two or more alternatives, and each of these alternatives has to be a realistic possibility. It is unusual for a healthcare decision maker to consider offering placebo as a therapy option. Therefore, placebo is rarely an appropriate comparator in an economic evaluation. That is, it is generally of little use to decision makers to know whether a particular therapy is more or less cost-effective than placebo. Along these same lines, it is often helpful to include a comparison to present care (or usual, standard, or routine care) to allow a clear assessment of whether moving from where an organization is at present (i.e., offering the present form of care) to some alternative makes sense. The choice and definition of appropriate comparators is discussed further in Chapter 4.

Timeliness and relevance. For economic evaluation to have a primary purpose as a decision making tool, it must be timely and relevant. The information must be available to decision makers in time for it to be of use to the decision—e.g., before the budget is due. Therefore, an economic evaluation must be practical, and have the overall goal of providing the best information available within the timeframe available. The information must also be relevant to that decision maker and decision. The economic evaluation must use unit costs that are comparable to those faced by the decision maker, and compare alternatives which are feasible and of interest—e.g., usual care should represent what is usual for that decision maker's situation.[11]

Second principle: incremental analysis

In the simplest sense, an economic evaluation involves the comparison of benefits to costs, and allows consideration of whether the benefits achieved are worth the costs incurred. However, in making this comparison it is important to realize that the real question being asked is: are the additional benefits of one option over another worth the additional costs of that option over the other? In other words, are the *incremental* (or net) benefits of one option over another worth the *incremental* (or net) costs? An economic evaluation always assumes that the decision maker is in one situation (e.g., a health plan covers a particular set of procedures for back pain, or a hospital offers a particular set of therapies) and is considering whether to change this situation (e.g., by adding coverage for a new procedure, or replacing one therapy with another). Therefore, it is the cost (and effect) of that *change* that is important.

As an example, Table 1 presents the results of a 2004 economic evaluation comparing usual general practitioner (GP) care alone to the addition of osteopathic spinal manipulation for subacute back pain.[12] Although one could compare the simple ratios of costs to outcomes for each arm of the study, the correct comparison is that of incremental costs to incremental outcomes. This tells how much we are paying, for each additional quality-adjusted life-year (QALY) gained, to add osteopathy. In brief, a QALY adjusts each year of life by the health-related quality of life experienced during that period. A year of life under perfect health has a value of 1.0, and death has a value of 0.0. Therefore, the relevant cost per QALY for the addition of osteopathy is £3,560, not £5,411 per QALY. The decision makers in this example (the United Kingdom's National Health Service - NHS) were already getting a gain (over baseline) of 0.031 QALYs per patient at a cost per QALY of £6,935. Their question is: how much do the 0.025 *additional* QALYs gained from adding osteopathy cost? They cost £88 per patient, or £3,560 per QALY. It is now up to the NHS to decide whether this amount is cost-effective (i.e., whether the health gains are worth the cost).

Table 1. Economic evaluation of adding osteopathy to usual general practitioner (GP) care for subacute back pain

	Cost	Health outcome (QALY gain)	Ratio of cost to outcome (£/QALY)*
Usual care	£215	0.031	£6,935
Usual care plus osteopathy	£303	0.056	£5,411
Increment of the addition of osteopathy over usual care alone	£88	0.025	£3,560

QALY = quality-adjusted life-year
Costs are reported for fiscal year 1999/2000.
* The first two numbers in this column were calculated from numbers available in the published article. The last number in this column was taken directly from the article and was apparently calculated using a cost and/or QALY estimate with more decimal places than reported in the article. Nevertheless, the relative sizes of these cost estimates are still valid for explanatory purposes.
Source: Williams et al (2004).[12]

Third principle: perspective of the analysis

This principle calls attention to one of the first challenges in determining the costs to include in an economic evaluation: whose view (*perspective*) of costs should be used? For example, the cost of acupuncture is different if you are a hospital, a health plan, or a patient. The cost of acupuncture from the perspective of the hospital would include the cost of the needles and the space needed to offer the service, plus the cost to pay the acupuncturist and any staff needed for scheduling. The cost of acupuncture from the point of view of the health plan would include the amount reimbursed for each acupuncture session. The cost of acupuncture from the patient's perspective would be the amount he or she would have to pay out-of-pocket for each session plus the time and expense incurred in getting to the appointment.

In general, the perspective of the analysis is determined by the identity of the decision maker the economic evaluation is intended to inform. If the purpose of the economic evaluation is to provide information to health plans on whether it makes sense to provide coverage for a particular therapy, then that economic evaluation should be performed from the perspective of a health plan (aka the third-party payer perspective). It should be noted that many economic evaluations contain results from more than one perspective, and, thus, are useful to more than one type of decision maker. In practice, much of the data collection and analysis required for one perspective can also serve to produce results relevant to another perspective. This is especially true of the societal perspective which captures all costs no matter who pays.

There are as many possible perspectives as there are decision makers. However, the most common perspectives used in published studies are those of the third-party payer (e.g., health insurance companies), hospital, employer, or society as a whole. The societal perspective accumulates all outcomes, while the others are more selective. Examples of the costs included for each perspective are presented in Chapter 3.

The Panel on Cost Effectiveness in Health and Medicine, appointed by the US Public Health Service, recommends that all economic evaluations include a "reference case" analysis from the societal perspective.[13] The Panel argues that the societal perspective is in line with the view that decisions are most likely fair when they are made in the public interest, and not in the interest of those who would directly gain or lose. The Panel goes on to say that the societal perspective "is the only perspective that never counts as a gain what is really someone else's loss."[13, p7] Ideally, decision makers who are establishing state or national healthcare policy would take the societal perspective because they are concerned with the impact of a healthcare decision on all their constituents.

One perspective that is rarely used in published economic evaluations of healthcare is that of the patient. The costs to the patient are included in the societal perspective, but since much of CIM depends on patient self-referral, and given increasing interest in patient-centered healthcare, separate reporting of results from the patient perspective makes sense. These results can give an indication of an option's relative attractiveness to patients. Also, explicit consideration of the patient perspective will help ensure that the societal perspective truly contains all costs.

A final point is that although the perspective mainly determines the costs to use in an economic evaluation, it is also important that the health benefits (or effects) measured are of interest to the decision maker. For example, a government official may be interested in the cost of broad health improvements such as are measured by quality-adjusted life-years (QALYs), however, a hospital administrator may not be. Instead, a hospital administrator may be most interested in having beds available. Therefore, an economic evaluation aimed at informing this administrator might report results in terms of the cost per day of hospital stay reduced, rather than per QALY gained.

Fourth principle: the type of economic evaluation

There are a number of different types of economic evaluation. The main types of *full* economic evaluations are cost-effectiveness analysis (CEA), cost-utility analysis (CUA) and cost-benefit analysis (CBA). These differ mainly in the manner in which health impacts are measured and included. If the health impacts are measured in some standard natural unit such as years of life saved, or percentage point reductions in hemoglobin A1c (HbA1c), then the economic evaluation is a cost-effectiveness analysis. If health impacts are measured more broadly in terms such as quality-adjusted life-years (QALYs), then it is a cost-utility analysis. However, if the health impact has been monetized (e.g., given a dollar value) using a human capital or "willingness to pay" type method, then it is a cost-benefit analysis. There is also one other type of economic evaluation (cost consequence analysis or CCA) which may be especially useful to CIM. It presents all costs and outcomes for each alternative and leaves it to the decision maker to choose those that are most relevant. The choice of health outcomes best suited for each type of evaluation is explored in Chapter 6.

Cost-effectiveness analyses (CEA) are the most common type of economic evaluation found in the literature. One reason is because a CEA can directly use the health outcome units measured in the effectiveness trial(s). If the health outcome is a widely accepted clinical measure for a particular disease or condition, cost-effectiveness analysis results using that outcome can then be directly compared across therapy options for that disease or condition. For example, various options to lower HbA1c could all be directly compared using CEA results in terms of a cost per percentage point reduction in HbA1c. The disadvantage of using CEA is that it does not allow direct cost comparisons across healthcare options available for different diseases. Also, of particular concern for CIM, CEA would allocate all costs to just one of what could be many different types of health effects seen. For example, a CIM therapy targeting diabetes may not only lower HbA1c, but also improve blood lipids, sleep, and overall energy.

Examples of CIM studies using different health outcomes in CEA include; cost per reduction in percent breech presentations at delivery for pregnant women who were given moxibustion of acupuncture point Zhiyin (Bladder 67);[14] cost per days free of back pain and/or Roland disability score change from the Alexander technique or massage;[15] and cost per hip fracture avoided in a study of Tai Chi for nursing home residents.[16]

Cost-utility analyses (CUA) are intended to improve upon the limitations of CEA by incorporating a broad measure of health. This broad measure of health attempts to incorporate all aspects of health (or its opposite, disease or morbidity) and mortality, and allows direct comparisons across all types of therapies targeting all types of health states. Because CUAs use a broad measure of health, they are an especially good type of economic evaluation for CIM. "Utilities" in health economics "are numbers that represent the strength of an individual's preference for different health outcomes under conditions of uncertainty."[17, p241] The conventional utility scale allocates a utility of 1.0 for complete or perfect health, and 0.0 for being dead. States worse than death can have negative utility values. Utility scores are used as the preference or quality-of-life weights when calculating QALYs. The reference case recommended by the US Panel on Cost Effectiveness in Health and Medicine is a CUA from the societal perspective using QALYs as the measure of health outcomes.[18] More information on the measurement of QALYs is discussed in Chapter 6. Note that there can be problems with interpretation of utilities and that many utility measures are in various stages of development, so it is sometimes recommended that both CEA and CUA results be presented.[19]

Examples of CUA in CIM include the series of studies of acupuncture for various conditions (chronic low back pain, headache, dysmenorrhea, and allergic rhinitis), each of which reported a cost per QALY from the societal perspective.[20-24]

Cost-benefit analyses (CBA) include all costs and benefits in monetary terms. In the ideal sense, CBAs have three advantages. The first is that costs can be directly subtracted from benefits to give the net monetary benefit of one option over another. The second is that like CUAs, a CBA should be able to incorporate the monetary value of all the health benefits of an option and to allow comparisons across therapies targeting different disease states. The third is that a CBA should also be able to incorporate non-health related benefits—e.g., the value of patient empowerment. These last two advantages should make CBA the economic evaluation of choice for CIM.[5] However, the big disadvantage of CBAs is that they require that a monetary value be put on health—and on all other outcomes. Monetizing health is morally problematic for many people. Therefore, few

CBAs have been done in healthcare.[25] In fact, CBA has been called "a formulation in search of data."[26,p212] No CBAs of CIM from a societal perspective were found in a recent search. However, the following could be an example of a CBA from the employer perspective: costs compared to the health benefit to employers of naturopathic care for chronic low back pain.[27] The health benefit was measured as reduced absentee days, which were then valued using the cost to the employer (in terms of salary and benefits—i.e., using a human capital approach) of each absentee day.

Cost-consequence analysis (CCA) is a form of full economic evaluation that makes few assumptions and places the greatest burden on the user of the analysis.[17] This analysis lists the cost components and various outcomes of each therapy separately, leaving it to the decision maker to prioritize and choose the costs and outcomes of most interest from his or her point of view. In this way a CCA can be considered to be a method for reporting the results of a full economic evaluation. Because of the broad range of health and other outcomes seen in CIM, CCA seems particularly suited to these evaluations. Using CCA, individual health impacts (e.g., biomarkers and reports of function improvement for the health condition of interest, as well as other positive side effects such as improvements in cognitive function, energy, pain, sleep, mood, well-being, etc.), and summary measures (e.g., QALYs) can each be listed for each therapy. This allows the decision maker to both see the range of benefits offered by and cost impacts of CIM, and to note those of most interest and relevance to the decision at hand. It is recommended that all economic evaluations of CIM report their outcomes in terms of a CCA, whether or not the analysis goes on to report specific CEA, CUA, or CBA results under one or more perspectives.

An example of a CCA of CIM is an economic evaluation which compared treatment by a musculoskeletal medicine physician (using acupuncture, manual therapy, injections and other pain management techniques) to management by an orthopedic surgeon-led team for patients with 'non-surgical' musculoskeletal conditions (e.g., low back pain and soft tissue knee injuries).[28] The report lists the number and cost of each type of individual treatment given, and a number of different health outcomes for each group.

Other types of economic evaluation. There are a number of other types of studies which include costs, but are not full economic evaluations. CEA, CUA, and CBA are all considered forms of full economic evaluations because they compare costs and health effects between two or more therapies.

Cost minimization analysis (CMA) includes an explicit assumption that the health impacts of the therapies compared are equivalent, therefore, CMA has been called a full economic evaluation.[29] However, it is no longer regarded as such.[26, p12] Instead, it is now considered to be a *partial* economic evaluation. Other types of partial economic evaluations include cost outcome descriptions, which consider the costs and health outcomes of only one therapy (i.e., no comparison), and cost comparisons which compare only costs between two or more healthcare options.[25,26] Many cost comparisons have been mistakenly called CBAs because they include monetized values.[25] However, because they lack a measure of health benefit, they are partial economic evaluations and not CBAs.

A study which described the diagnoses, prescriptions and costs of patients seen by a sample of French homeopathic general practitioners is an example of a CIM cost outcome description.[30] An example of a cost comparison evaluation in CIM is a study that used claims data to determine and compare the costs reimbursed per patient for physicians in Switzerland who were certified to practice homeopathy, anthroposophic medicine, neural therapy, and/or traditional Chinese medicine to those who were not.[31]

Final points. Because the type of economic evaluation mainly differs in the form in which the health effects are reported, more than one type can be reported in one study. For example, it is common that both CEA and CUA results are presented. Also, it is common in the literature for CEA, CUA, and CBA to be mislabeled,[25] and for the terms cost-effectiveness analysis and cost-benefit analysis to be used as general terms each encompassing all types of economic evaluation. Finally, as noted above in the third principle, the perspective of the analysis mainly determines the costs to include in an economic evaluation. However, perspective should also be considered when determining the appropriate form of the health benefits, and thus, the type of economic evaluation performed.

CHAPTER 3. COSTS

The defining element of an economic evaluation is cost. Most people consider cost to be synonymous with price—e.g., asking a sales clerk, how much does this cost? A price is the amount of money set by the seller (or actually paid to the seller) for the purchase of something. In economic terms cost is both a much broader and more specific concept. Several aspects of cost are discussed below, which may help the reader better understand the concept of cost as it is used in an economic evaluation.

Input and consequence/outcome costs

When considering the cost of massage for low back pain, for example, the concept of cost needs to be broken down into two main components. There are the costs of providing the massage itself (e.g., salary paid to the massage therapist, cost of the massage oil, administrative costs in scheduling the appointment, and cost of the room and its furnishings). These are considered up-front, input, or intervention costs. Then there are the costs resulting from what happens to the person's health because of the massage, which can be increases or decreases (i.e., savings). These are cost (or economic) consequences (or outcomes), and can include things like increased medical costs to address side effects, decreased medical costs because improved health leads to lower healthcare utilization, and improved work productivity because of better health. The point here is that an economic evaluation should include both the costs to provide the therapy in the first place, and the costs (or cost savings) of what happens because of the therapy.

Technically, one can perform an economic evaluation that only considers input costs. Note that since much of CIM is used in addition to usual care, this will inevitably result in showing a cost increase for CIM—i.e., showing CIM only as an "add-on" expense. However, many CIM therapies have been shown to improve health, which then results in lower overall healthcare utilization and other costs later, making the measurement of economic outcomes especially important for CIM. See Box 1 for an example.

> *Box 1.*
>
> A 2006 study by Ratcliffe et al32,33 compared the costs and health benefits of the addition of up to 10 individualized sessions with a Traditional Chinese Medicine-trained acupuncturist in a private acupuncture clinic to usual care alone for patients with low back pain. The course of acupuncture treatment costs an average of £214 per patient to administer. Over the next two years direct healthcare costs for the acupuncture group totaled £246 per patient. Direct healthcare costs for the usual care-only group over the two years averaged £345. Therefore, the addition of acupuncture at a cost of £214 per patient saved an average of £99 per patient in other healthcare costs. From the payer perspective this results in a cost increase for acupuncture, but it is an increase of £115 per patient (£214 - £99) rather than the full £214. From the societal perspective, including patient out-of-pocket costs and reductions in productivity losses for employers, the results look even better. Unfortunately, the study did not report out-of-pocket costs and productivity losses separately or by group. However, when these costs are included, the acupuncture group showed net savings of an average of £248 per patient compared to usual care alone.

Direct (medical and non-medical) and indirect costs

Costs can also be categorized as direct or indirect costs. Direct costs are said to be "wholly attributable to the use of the healthcare intervention in question."[17, p50] Direct costs include medical and non-medical costs. Medical costs are all costs related to the healthcare system and include practitioner and staff time, facilities, medications, devices, etc. Non-medical costs are, for the most part, healthcare-related costs incurred by the patient as a result of the intervention. The best examples of these are transportation costs to and from appointments or classes, the patient's time involved in receiving care, and childcare costs. However, it may also be appropriate to include other expenses specific to the intervention—e.g., purchase of a yoga mat required for a yoga class intervention. Note that direct costs include both input costs and economic consequences (from above).

Indirect costs in economic evaluations of healthcare almost exclusively refer to gains or losses in work productivity due to the intervention. Note that these gains or losses are specifically savings or costs to employers and to others who would have benefited from the individual's productivity.

Both would be included in the societal perspective, and productivity loss to employers would be included in the employer perspective. However, the gains or losses to the individual (e.g., in terms of income) are not generally counted as costs. They are assumed to be captured in the measure of quality of life (e.g., QALYs). Indirect costs and productivity will be further discussed below as they relate to the societal perspective and in Chapter 5.

Resource use multiplied by unit cost

Although we tend to automatically think of cost in monetary terms, it is actually more appropriate and clear-cut, to think of cost in terms of the value of resources expended or saved.[34] Resources such as staff time, medications, supplements, office visits, and facilities are used up in providing a therapy and/or are saved (not used when they otherwise would have been) because of the success of the therapy. In an economic evaluation, it is the change in use of each of these resources that is measured. Measurements should be made in appropriate units —e.g., hours of staff time, or numbers of regular office visits.

This change in resource use is then valued by multiplying each by its unit cost—e.g., the increase in staff hours multiplied by the hourly wage paid. The appropriate unit cost to use in each case is the opportunity cost (see below) for that resource.

Opportunity cost

"The opportunity cost of using a resource in a given activity is the value/benefit/return/compensation that must be foregone because the resource is not available for use in the next best option."[17, p52] In most cases the opportunity cost of using a resource will equal its usual price (or in the case of staff time, the going salary or wage rate plus benefits).[35] For example, the opportunity cost of a box of acupuncture needles will most likely be the price paid for the needles, say $10 per box. The 'next best option' for these acupuncture needles could be their use on patients in some other clinic, but because they were used for your intervention, they are no longer available for use in the other clinic. Presumably, the other clinic would also have been willing to pay $10 for this box of needles. Therefore, $10 in resource value was "foregone" (i.e., used up) because the needles were used and not available to the other clinic.

Although the concept of opportunity cost requires what might seem like convoluted thinking, it becomes clearer when considering cases when the opportunity cost is not equal to a resource's price. Consider the following examples, one where the opportunity cost is lower than the price (or going rate), and one where it is higher than the price. If a yoga class uses a classroom in a facility only during hours when that classroom was otherwise empty, and if there were no other uses available for that open time in that space, the opportunity cost of that classroom space can be argued to be $0 rather than, for example, the going rate for leasing classroom space. The next best option for that classroom is to be empty, therefore, there is no value foregone by using it for the yoga class. On the other hand, if a clinic utilizes unpaid volunteers to greet patients, by definition their price (or wage rate) is $0. However, the next best option for the volunteers' time cannot be said to have no value. The volunteers could offer their time somewhere else, which would be of value to those at that other location. The volunteers could also elect to have more leisure time, which would provide them with value. It is usual in an economic evaluation to set the opportunity cost of volunteer time at some average wage rate in order to acknowledge the value of this resource.[18, p201]

The costs to include for each perspective

The actual cost components to include in the evaluation of any particular therapy for any particular health condition will vary both due to the data collection situation (see next section), and the perspective of the analysis. Table 2 gives an overview of the cost categories to consider in an economic evaluation.

Table 2. Cost components to include in an economic evaluation

Type of cost	Examples	Perspective in which this cost is included
Direct medical costs	Outpatient visit costs (for both conventional and CIM practitioners; can be included as an overall visit cost or may be built up from individual cost components such as staff time, materials, and facility costs) Medication costs (can include over-the-counter medications and	The portion covered by health insurance is included in the third-party payer perspective. The portion paid by the employer is included in the employer perspective. Costs which are the responsibility of the hospital are included in the hospital perspective.

Type of cost	Examples	Perspective in which this cost is included
	supplements as well as prescriptions) Lab and imaging costs ED visit costs Hospital stay costs	The portion paid out-of-pocket by the patient is included in the patient perspective. All are included in the societal perspective.
Direct non-medical costs	Transportation costs to and from the intervention Patient's time in receiving care Childcare costs incurred during appointments Other intervention-related costs—e.g., the cost of a yoga mat for a yoga intervention or a gym membership if recommended by the intervention	Usually these costs are all paid by the patient, so are included in the patient perspective. All are included in the societal perspective.
Indirect costs	Lost work productivity due to deterioration of health state	Included in the employer perspective. Included in the societal perspective.

While the US Panel on Cost-Effectiveness in Health and Medicine recommends that in order to be most useful to decision makers all economic evaluations should contain a "reference case" CUA from the societal perspective,[18, p11] various researchers have discovered that, in practice, there is little agreement as to exactly what all should be included in this perspective.[36,37] According to Weinstein et al, from a societal perspective the "costs and consequences of health interventions may include increases or decreases in any or all of the following: mortality, health-related quality of life, time spent receiving or delivering health services, productive output, and enjoyment of leisure time."[38, p 506] In general, the first two components, mortality and health-related quality of life, are captured in health effects when a summary measure such as QALYs is used. However, some aspects of these components could be included as costs, although they usually are not—e.g., the loss of quality of life and productivity of friends and family due to the death or loss of function of the individual under treatment. We regularly capture the time spent by physicians and other healthcare workers in delivering health services by including changes in health care utilization in costs. However, the opportunity costs, in terms of lost work or leisure, of time spent by family members in giving care and of the individual in receiving care should also be counted, but rarely are. The time cost of receiving care should be considered when patient time commitments differ between options, and the patient perspective is considered. Patient time costs can be substantial, and may provide information on the patient's choice of treatment.[39]

Most of the confusion regarding the societal perspective seems to come from the inclusion of productivity losses. It is important to recognize that the impact of changes in productive output to society has at least three parts: the loss of income to the individual whose productivity is affected; the external consumption losses to the rest of society; and productivity losses to the employer. Much of the discussion in the literature focuses on the first of these, income-mediated losses to the individual (see, for example, Tilling et al[40] for a review). The US Panel has argued that these losses are captured in QALYs.[18,38] However, it has also been argued that if clear instructions are given to ignore income losses (which is not often done)when preference weights for QALYs are determined, then income losses to individuals can be included in costs.[41] The losses to the rest of society can be most easily illustrated by the loss of taxes paid by the individual, or an increase in disability payments, and are rarely captured.[38,41] The cost of productivity losses to the employer are appropriate to include and will be discussed in more detail in Chapter 5. Note that these productivity losses are not losses to the individual, and therefore are not included in the patient perspective. Instead, they are the losses to the employer, and are included in the employer and societal perspective.

How to identify the costs to include in an economic evaluation

The easiest way to determine which costs should and should not be included in an economic evaluation is to place yourself in the shoes of the decision maker at the point in time when the result of the decision will begin.[35,42] For example, imagine you are a hospital administrator tasked with determining whether or not you should start making music therapy available to your pediatric patients who are undergoing ECG (electrocardiogram) procedures.[43] Let's say your decision will take effect at the beginning of the next budget cycle, July 1st. To determine the costs to include in an economic evaluation, consider the post-July 1st future if you continue with your present protocols for pediatric ECG and compare it to the future if you add music therapy. What will be different? How will clinical processes change and how will that affect resource use?[35]

In general the costs to *include* are those that are relevant to the decision maker (see Table 2) and that are expected to be different between the two arms of the study. In our example, the costs to include are those that are expected to be noticeably different for the hospital between a future of usual care versus a future of usual care plus music therapy.[42] The costs to *collect during the trial* are those that would vary from patient to patient (i.e., if a cost is known and doesn't vary then it can be added in later), and that would be costly to collect retrospectively or in parallel (e.g., things not typically found in patient records such as medical and nursing time).[44,45] In the music therapy example, the amount of time the music therapist spends with each patient may vary and would only occur in one arm of the study. Therefore, it should be measured during the study. Any expected differences between study arms in the time requirements per procedure of other staff (e.g., nursing and the ECG technician) and in the amount and type of medications needed should also be measured real-time. However, the upfront cost of any equipment the music therapist may need would not vary from patient to patient. This cost would only be included in the music therapy study arm, but it would not require ongoing data collection during the trial. The study should, where possible, collect information on all resource use, not just that considered disease- or intervention-related.[42,46,47] This is especially important for CIM interventions, which can affect more than just targeted costs. The distinction between costs related and unrelated to the disease/intervention should be made during the design phase if possible, and addressed in the sensitivity analysis.

Two other considerations also come into play when deciding exactly which costs to include. Generally, it is more important to measure and include the big costs (either large individual costs, or small costs that occur a large number of times) than the small costs.[42] That is, *a priori* estimation of relative importance of costs should guide data collection. This is an especially important consideration when some costs are more difficult to capture (i.e., more expensive to measure) than others. The second consideration is the length of time costs should be tracked. Generally, the appropriate follow-up period for costs should be the same as for the health impacts,[42] and "is up to the analyst so long as the result does not mislead the decision maker or user."[17, p52] This recommendation offers guidance for both the choice of costs and the choice of a follow-up period—neither should bias the analysis in favor of one intervention over another.

Finally, an economic evaluation should itself be cost-effective.[44] The benefits gained from having the results of the evaluation should be worth the additional costs of performing the evaluation. This tenet should be applied both to the decision to undertake an economic evaluation, and to decisions as to the level of detail to include at each step. It is usually worthwhile to perform an economic evaluation, and, once the data are available, it is almost always worthwhile to do the best analysis and reporting of the results as possible.

CHAPTER 4. ECONOMIC EVALUATION STUDY DESIGNS

There are three main ways to perform an economic evaluation and each is appropriate and feasible in different situations and under different conditions. These are summarized in Table 3 and each is discussed below.

Table 3. Study designs used for economic evaluation

	Alongside a clinical trial	Using observational data	Simulation or decision analytic modeling
Commonly used?	Most common for CIM	Common in both conventional and CIM	Most common for conventional medicine
Key requirements	An appropriate clinical trial in the planning stages	Retrospective: data source(s) containing all needed inputs Prospective: above or the ability to obtain other needed data from participants	Published evidence on effectiveness, and published evidence on costs or the ability to estimate costs through other means
Expense and effort	Inexpensive if added to appropriate trial; long lead times to results	Expense and timing depends on availability of data and whether retrospective or prospective	Less expensive than a trial, simpler models can be built in a year

Economic evaluation alongside a clinical trial

The first method is to gather economic data alongside a clinical trial. This, of course, requires that a clinical trial is being planned, and that the trial design is appropriate for an economic evaluation (more on this below). This is the most common method used for economic evaluations of CIM.[48] There are advantages and disadvantages to performing economic evaluation within the constructs of a clinical trial, and much has been written on this topic. As is indicative of their name (economic evaluation alongside a clinical trial or "piggyback" economic evaluation), these types of evaluations are rarely the primary purpose of the trial. Nevertheless, if this approach is undertaken, it is important for the health economic analyst to be involved early and contribute to the design of the trial to ensure that it provides the data necessary for a high-quality economic study.[42]

Advantages

There are two major advantages to adding an economic evaluation to an existing planned trial. The economic evaluation benefits from the internal validity and quality of the data produced by the trial. Since an economic evaluation is dependent on the quality of the underlying medical evidence, clinical trials have been considered to be the natural vehicle for economic analysis.[11,44,45] The second advantage is that the costs of adding an economic evaluation to a trial are usually low.[11] However, "[t]here is no point in wasting resources in undertaking economic analysis alongside poorly designed trials."[44, p1403] It is generally acknowledged that pragmatic effectiveness trials are the best vehicles for economic studies.[42] These trials will be discussed in more detail below in terms of specific trial design issues, but for more information about the difference between effectiveness and efficacy, and the corresponding difference between pragmatic and explanatory trials, please see Thorpe et al (2009) on the pragmatic-explanatory continuum, and Tunis et al (2003) on the usefulness of pragmatic trials for decision making.[49,50]

Issues in trial design

There are several issues regarding the design of a clinical trial that makes it more or less appropriate for the addition of an economic evaluation. These include the selection of an appropriate comparator, sample size, study duration, and length and timing of follow up.

Comparators. The interventions being compared in the study need to be as close as possible to real choices facing healthcare decision makers.[11,45,47]

For an economic evaluation, it is best if the trial compares the intervention(s) to a control group representing usual, routine, or best-alternative treatment.[11,44,47] Placebo is only suitable for economic evaluation if the no-treatment option reflects the best alternative action, and if the administration of placebo has a minimal impact on the process of patient care (i.e., the dispensing of placebo is not so obvious to patients and practitioners that they are likely to respond differently than they would to no treatment).[11,44,47]

Since CIM therapies can range from the substitution of an herb for a pharmaceutical agent, to patients being seen in an integrative clinic rather than conventional primary care, it is important that all study comparators be defined (at least) to the level at which their differences end.[51] Basically in a study comparing two drugs, or a drug to an herbal product, all else is held equal. Often the same practitioner provides each option within the same clinic, and strict protocols ensure that the only difference is the content of the pills and safeguard treatment fidelity. There is no need (other than to establish a general context for the trial) to define the type of practitioner or their philosophy, or the clinic characteristics or the clinic's place in the overall healthcare system, because these are the same for both study arms. However, when two *systems* of medicine are compared, very little can be assumed to be held equal. Not only will different treatments be offered, but different practitioners with dramatically different training will diagnose and prescribe treatments in different clinical settings and under different philosophies of care. Some method of defining, and then measuring, the major characteristics of these medical systems is needed to ensure that both interventions (the CIM intervention and usual care) are implemented as intended—i.e., to ensure treatment fidelity. Basically, the more complex the intervention, the more work must be put into identifying what it is that is actually being compared. This defining and fidelity measurement should be done whether or not the trial adds an economic evaluation.

In many cases, the comparison in a trial is between usual care and usual care plus the addition of the CIM therapy. In this case, it could be argued that only the CIM therapy must be defined because everything else is equal—i.e., because both groups received usual care, the addition of the CIM therapy constitutes the only difference. It may be true that there is less of a need to define and measure usual care for the purposes of treatment fidelity. However, a good definition is still needed for study transferability, which is the closest economic evaluations get to generalizability (see

Chapter 8). The concept of treatment fidelity emerged in the 1960s in psychotherapy when early attempts to sort out design and interpretive problems in outcomes studies proved impossible. For a brief history and overview of treatment fidelity and its measurement, see Bond et al (2000).[52] Box 2 provides an example of an economic evaluation alongside a clinical trial that put considerable effort into defining its comparators.

Box 2.

In 2004, the United Kingdom Back pain Exercise and Manipulation (UK BEAM) trial team published the results of their clinical trial[53] and cost-effectiveness analysis.[54] In this trial "best care" in general practice was compared to the addition of exercise classes, spinal manipulation, or both. It is common that economic evaluations conducted alongside clinical trials are published separately, and after the results of the clinical trial. The economic evaluation article can then refer to the clinical trial article for more detail on study design and the health impacts measured. If the interventions are complex, which is common in CIM, there is often the need for additional early articles to lay out the details of the interventions, as was seen in this study.

To ensure uniform application of best care, the trial team invited all participating practitioners and support staff to training sessions on the application of the UK national acute back pain guidelines. They also provided the corresponding patient booklet (*The Back Pain Book*) to all participating patients and practice reception areas.[55] Physiotherapists with at least two years' experience were trained to deliver the exercise program, which had been developed from previous trials.[56,57] The exercise program used cognitive behavioral techniques and consisted of up to eight one-hour class sessions over four to eight weeks. A group of chiropractors, osteopathic physicians, and physical therapists worked together to agree upon a package of spinal manipulation techniques to use in the trial, and these were described in yet another article.[58] Equal numbers of these types of practitioners delivered up to eight 20-minute treatments to study participants over 12 weeks. Those in the combined group were invited to get up to eight manipulation sessions over six weeks, and up to eight exercise classes over the next six weeks.

Unfortunately, no information was available in the published studies as to whether treatment fidelity was assessed.

Often, patients in clinical trials are more closely monitored than in regular practice (i.e., usual care), so more clinical problems are detected and possibly resolved than in real practice.[45,47] Along this line, it is important to identify resource use that was due solely to the trial itself. [45,47,59] For example, the trial protocol may result in either more or fewer tests (and other resource use) than seen in actual practice. The economic evaluation must carefully adjust for these trial-only costs.[45,47]

Sample size. The sample size for a clinical trial is usually determined by the number needed to give statistical significance to a clinically significant change. [45,47] Economic outcomes may require larger sample sizes because of the greater variability seen in many of these variables—e.g., due to rare, random, high-cost items such as hospitalizations.[19,47] However, a trial large enough for statistical significance in the economic outcomes may not be feasible, and it may not be ethical to enroll more patients than necessary for clinical significance.[47] Ideally, economic outcomes would be factored into sample size calculations. However, it is common for sample size to be determined by clinical outcomes alone.[42] Note that according to one review: "none of the [economics] working groups suggested that the size of the proposed trial should be increased in order to increase the statistical power of the economic analysis."[19, p1419] In many cases, sample-size restrictions will necessitate focus on estimation rather than hypothesis testing of the economic outcomes.[42] It has been suggested that, even when cost or effectiveness outcomes are not statistically significant, a cost-effectiveness ratio should be presented along with confidence intervals (however wide) so that studies that are not adequately powered for the endpoints will not be misleading.[47] Uncertainty in economic evaluations can also be handled through methods other than statistical significance, as discussed in Chapter 7.

Study duration, and length and timing of follow up. The appropriate time horizon for an economic evaluation is one that is sufficiently long to reflect all the key differences between options in terms of costs and effects.[60] Therefore, an economic evaluation would like to have life-long follow up when the intervention has a life-long influence on survival.[11,19,42,47] In some trials, patients are only followed until a clinical event (e.g., a heart attack) occurs.[47] For an economic evaluation, all patients should be followed for a common length of time or the full duration of the trial.[42] It is understood that it is not always feasible to extend the study beyond an initial or relatively short-term follow up. In these cases it is possible to use modeling approaches to link final outcomes with the more intermediate outcomes gathered during the trial. [19,42,47] In practice, the appropriate follow-up period for a trial depends on the relationship between intermediate end points gathered during the trial, and long-term disease outcomes—the stronger that relationship, the more a reliance on intermediate end points can be justified. An economic evaluation may also require additional intermediate follow-up visits if cost data are dependent on self-report. Limits on participant memory recall necessitate relatively short periods between data collection points.[19] The use of self-report to collect data on resource use and costs is discussed in Chapter 5.

Outcomes measured. The choice of primary end point in a clinical study may not correspond with the ideal end point for economic evaluation. In the end, what is needed for economic evaluation is clinically meaningful (and thus, cost-relevant) disease end points.[42] Also, see the discussion of the choice of health outcomes in Chapter 6.

Economic evaluations based on observational data

In an observational study, patient's care is determined by means other than the study investigator—i.e., patients are not randomized. Observational studies can be either prospective (i.e., designed at one point and then data are collected from that point forward) or retrospective (i.e., designed to use data that have already been collected), and they are the second most common type of economic evaluation in CIM. In general, these studies are based upon data available in health plan claims databases and/or patients' medical charts/records.

The main benefit of an observational study is that the data collected will more likely represent real world care, free of the artificial effects of randomization. The main challenge faced by these studies is one of internal validity—i.e., can we assume that the differences seen between the treatment and control groups are solely due to the intervention. An additional challenge for retrospective studies is whether the data source(s) used contain all the information on costs and effects needed for an economic evaluation. Prospective studies have the opportunity to put data collection procedures in place to ensure that all needed information is captured.

In general, observational studies need to consider some of the same issues as clinical trial-based economic evaluations. Almost by definition, in an observational study the comparison will be made between real world options, but there still needs to be some thought and effort given to describing those comparators. Also, consideration should be given to study duration and the outcomes measured. However, since these studies are usually undertaken for the sole purpose of economic evaluation (instead of the economics being an "add on"), the sample size will be determined jointly by data availability and the needs of the economic evaluation.

Internal validity

The concept of internal validity relates to the question of whether the treatment can be said to have caused the differences seen in outcomes between the two groups under study.[61, pp 53-63] If patients are randomized to treatment and control, this strengthens the likelihood that any differences seen between groups are due to (i.e., caused by) the treatment because all else should be equal (or at least equally probable). This is why randomization is said to strengthen a study's internal validity. Randomization, by definition, does not occur in observational studies. Patients usually self-select into treatment and the reasons for their selection may also directly or indirectly affect their outcomes. Therefore, other methods (such as the identification of matched controls) are needed to ensure internal validity. However, well-designed observational studies have been found to produce results comparable to those seen in randomized trials.[62,63] A full discussion of the threats to internal validity which can occur and the methods available to address each is beyond the scope of this handbook. However, there are good resources available, including *Experimental and Quasi-Experimental Designs for Generalized Causal Inference* by Shadish, Cook and Campbell (2002).[61]

Boxes 3 and 4 give examples of two economic evaluations of chiropractic care using prospective and retrospective observational studies, respectively.

Box 3.

Haas, Sharma and Stano (2005)64 compared costs, pain, functional disability and patient satisfaction between two cohorts of self-referring patients with low back pain of mechanical origin: those seen by chiropractors in chiropractic clinics, and those seen by medical doctors in general practice community clinics. Multiple regression was used to control for differences between groups at baseline for all health and economic outcomes. A number of independent variables were included in these regression models, including baseline symptom severity and patients' reported difference in trust between chiropractors and MDs. The trust variable had been found to be predictive in choice of provider type in a previous study. Health outcomes for each cohort were measured using self-report instruments. Cost outcomes were based on resource use (e.g., visits and procedures) data gathered through a chart audit and valued using Medicare-based unit costs. Cost estimates from the literature were used for resource use not available from charts—e.g., advanced imaging, surgical consultation, and referrals to physical therapists.

Box 4.

A 2004 cost-comparison study by Legorreta and others[65] compared the overall costs of care between members of the same health plan who did or did not have a chiropractic care benefit rider. The study took advantage of a natural experiment where access to covered chiropractic care depended on the member's employer. Only claims data were used in the analysis, so health outcomes were not available. In order to maximize comparability between the two groups, a panel of chiropractic and medical neuro-musculoskeletal specialists was used to define diagnosis codes that would be equally applicable to both types of care, and these codes were used to select cases and to define episodes of care. In addition, regression was used to adjust for differences in co-morbidities and age between groups.

Economic evaluations via modeling

Most published economic evaluations in conventional medicine utilize mathematical modeling. The use of models for economic evaluations of CIM is increasing, but is still relatively rare.

Mathematical modeling is routinely used in a wide variety of scientific disciplines. Models "are a way of representing the complexity of the real world in a more simple and comprehensible form."[66, p217] They allow synthesis of the best of all available data, and are extremely useful when true experiments are infeasible or impracticable, or to explore alternative scenarios. In economic evaluations of healthcare, modeling is used in two main situations: to estimate the longer-term impacts of interventions for which only short-term or intermediate outcomes are available from clinical trials; and when the relevant clinical trials have not yet been performed or did not include economic outcomes.[66] Other situations in which modeling can be useful include: generalizing from efficacy to routine effectiveness; transferring evidence from one setting or country to another; and identifying where additional research is needed (i.e., gaps in knowledge), and how much that additional information is worth.[67] Box 5 gives an example of an economic evaluation of CIM using modeling.

Box 5.

The stated purpose of the economic modeling study of the addition of acupuncture to usual care for chronic low back pain (Kim et al 2010) includes "to provide information about the level of improvement required to substantially alter the cost-effectiveness of the therapeutic decision in South Korea."[68, p2] This study used modeling to adjust the results of studies performed elsewhere to be applicable for decisions in South Korea. A systematic review was performed as part of the study to capture data with which to parameterize a Markov model. The model used a hypothetical cohort of 10,000 60-year old women, a group with the highest prevalence of first experience of acute low back pain in Korea, and cycled them through the model. Each patient started from an initial state of acute low back pain and could go from there to chronic low back pain (if pain lasted more than 3 months), or to a well state (if they recovered). Those in the chronic low back pain state could also transition to the well state if they recovered, but if the pain recurred they would be transferred back to the chronic pain state. Cases in all states could be transferred to the death state based on Korean age- and sex-specific all-cause mortality rates. Movement from one state to another was based on a set of transition probabilities and each state had a corresponding utility (QALY) and cost estimate. The transition probabilities, costs and QALY estimates all came from the literature and/or systematic review. Individuals had a chance to move from one state to another every 3 months and the model was run for 20 cycles (5 years). The model was run once with transition probabilities based on usual care alone and once with the probabilities reflecting the addition of acupuncture. The results of the two models were then compared.

It is beyond the scope of this handbook to explain the process of economic modeling. Instead the reader interested in building a model or understanding a published study based on a model is referred to Weinstein and O'Brien (2003) on best practices for modeling[69] and Briggs et al (2006) on decision analytic modeling.[60]

Chapter 5. Measurement of costs

There are five main sources for data on costs for an economic evaluation: study records, administrative data, self-report, published sources, and expert opinion. Any particular economic evaluation will use one, or more likely a combination, of these to capture estimates of costs. Each is discussed below with reference to the types of studies likely to use these data. Of course, the specific costs to measure and include in an economic evaluation depend on the perspective of the analysis as discussed in Chapter 3.

As previously noted, the measurement of costs is best thought of as the measurement of resource use to which unit costs are later applied. Sources for unit cost estimates are discussed in a separate section below, but the range of possible resource costing methods is mentioned here briefly because it can differ by data source. Resource costing can be described by a continuum from micro-costing to gross costing.[35,70] Micro-costing counts each individual healthcare service resource item consumed by each patient (e.g., each bottle of massage oil, laundry charge for massage table linens, hour of practitioner and staff time, square foot of treatment room space, etc.) and then applies a unit cost to each. At the other end of the spectrum, gross costing applies a cost to a bundle of health services—e.g., to an entire hospital stay, or to the full series of visits, tests and procedures utilized for an episode of low back pain. As can be imagined, micro-costing requires a large data collection effort, but results in a fairly accurate estimate of costs, whereas gross costing entails minimal data collection effort but offers a less specific estimate of costs. Any costing effort will lie somewhere on the continuum between micro- and gross costing depending on the level of bundling chosen for the measurement of resource use.

It is important to decide up-front whether total costs of care will be included, and whether disease- or intervention-specific costs can be isolated.[47] Theoretically, disease- or intervention-specific costs should be less variable (e.g., because clearly unrelated high-cost hospitalizations will not be included), and more indicative of the effects of the therapy under study than total costs. However, due to a whole person approach, CIM therapies may also have a broad effect on overall healthcare costs. Therefore, restricting costs to those directly targeted by the intervention may miss some of the potential benefits of CIM. In general, it is recommended that all costs be measured, and that a decision be made up front as to whether total or disease- or intervention-specific costs will be used in the main analysis, with the other addressed through sensitivity analysis. Methods to identify and separate out disease- or intervention-specific costs should be defined at study start.

Finally, it is important that the study consent form for a trial or prospective observational study specifically mention the collection of healthcare utilization or economic data from third-party databases, medical records, and/or self-report.[42]

Study records

Study records are useful in economic evaluations alongside clinical trials and prospective observational studies to capture data on the cost of the interventions themselves. This data source is especially important for economic evaluations of CIM, or of any intervention that lacks established reimbursement rates in the existing healthcare system. The level of detail needed in tracking resource use will depend on the level of disaggregation needed to get down to a market (or other defendable) price for that resource or bundle of resources.

If, for example, the intervention is a visit to a chiropractor, and there is a generally recognized standard price for a chiropractic visit (a visit similar to that offered in the intervention), then the only information needed from the study records is the actual number of visits each patient attended. It might also be appropriate to note scheduled visits which were missed without sufficient notice of cancellation, since these visits also have a cost if that visit slot cannot be filled due to the short notice.

If, instead, the intervention is a package of classes and visits to a new integrative medicine clinic, then more detailed resource use data might be needed to appropriately value the intervention. In this case, study records might need to capture the numbers and types of classes attended by each patient, and the staff time, materials, and facility space required to offer each of those classes as well as the length of visits and the time spent by each type of practitioner and other staff.

Earlier, the concept of defining each comparator in the study up to the level where their differences end was introduced as especially important for evaluations of CIM. Here we need to generate an input cost estimate for each of these comparators. The input cost estimates for each arm of the study should be comparable in terms of accuracy and credibility.

Administrative data

The term administrative data applies in this context to all data gathered for one purpose (usually to satisfy an administrative need such as billing) that may also be useful to an economic evaluation. These data sources include insurance claims data, hospital billing and other administrative data, clinic billing records and medical charts—both hard copy and electronic medical records. These data sources, particularly when available electronically, can provide an inexpensive, detailed accounting of the healthcare resources consumed by patients.[42] Because data from insurance claims and from medical charts are the two most common types of administrative data used in economic evaluations, they are discussed in more detail below. However, the issues raised for these will also generally be applicable to other types of administrative data.

Insurance claims data

Even though much of CIM is not covered by insurance,[3,71] economic evaluations of non-covered CIM can still benefit from claims data to track the use of other reimbursable healthcare. Claims data are germane for all types of economic evaluations. However, the requirements of these data differ depending on whether individual claims data must be matched to other patient data (i.e., connected to other self-report or medical record data for each patient), such as is required in economic evaluations alongside clinical trials and in some observational studies, or whether de-identified aggregate data are used, such as in a claims-data-only retrospective observational study (see, for example, Box 4) or a modeling study.

The use of individual claims data presents more of a challenge. It is really only feasible if all or most study patients give consent to having their claims data extracted, and if all or most patients are members of one or a small number of health plans (and those plans agree to provide information for consenting patients); or if patients are all employees of one employer who has access to employee claims data and who agrees to provide these data for consenting patients. Collecting claims data from a number of different health plans, even with patient consent, quickly becomes impractical both in terms of obtaining the data in a timely manner, and in terms of reconciling varying data formats and coding schemes across plans.

There are a number of sources for de-identified claims data which can be used in retrospective observational studies (if the health plan covers CIM) or in modeling studies. Individual health plans are often willing to sell de-identified data for research purposes. Other commercial organizations (e.g., MarketScan, Medi-Span, and the Health Care Cost Institute) collect claims from a variety of health plans, employers, and state-level Medicaid agencies. These large databases increase the scope of coverage represented, and the numbers, types, and distribution of individuals' data available to researchers. Information on each of these large datasets and their cost and requirements for purchase are available online at their websites.

No matter the source, there are generally three types of claims data available: medical (i.e., outpatient visits, ED services and hospitalizations), pharmacy and labs. The nature of individual claims is indicated through diagnosis codes (e.g., ICD-9 codes), procedure codes (e.g., CPT codes), or the drug class and name. Cost data include: the amount allowed (or the eligible amount; the amount the insurance company agrees that this resource is worth), the net payment (or amount paid; the amount that goes from the insurance company to the provider), and the patient's out-of-pocket cost (the amount the patient is responsible for through co-payments, deductibles or co-insurance; this should equal the difference between the previous two). If the economic evaluation uses the societal perspective, data from the first cost category (the amount allowed or eligible) are needed. In contrast, the payer perspective would mainly require data from the second category (the amount paid) and the patient perspective would mainly require data from the third (patient out-of-pocket). Sometimes the billed or charged amount is also available. This amount is usually larger than that termed allowed or eligible and generally should not be used in an economic evaluation, because it reflects charges (what the provider charges patients) rather than costs (the cost of the resources consumed).[72] Finally, although claims data arrive with costs attached, it is useful to the transferability ("generalizability") of economic evaluations to report resource use separately from unit costs. Therefore, the number of claims for a particular type of visit, procedure, or drug or lab test should be reported separately from the average cost per claim.

Medical chart data

Medical chart review is another accurate, albeit extremely expensive (especially in the absence of electronic medical records), method to collect resource use within an observational study. Because it is so time intensive, this method is less commonly used. However, as the use of electronic medical records becomes more widespread, and the data they contain more accessible, more economic evaluations will likely utilize this data source in the future. The two main challenges with retrospective medical chart review, which will likely still exist using an electronic medical record, are incomplete data (not everything that occurs and is of interest to an economic evaluation makes it into the chart), and inconsistent reporting (different terminology or units are used, and information is reported in different areas of the chart). These issues can, to some extent, be addressed in a prospective study where protocols are put in place or software code written to ensure complete and consistent data are recorded. However, they still require the initial and ongoing buy-in of all those who input data into that record. Box 3 provides an example of an economic evaluation that used data from a medical chart audit, patient self-report, and the literature.

Patient self-report

Patient self-report of resource use is generally unavoidable for economic evaluations of CIM alongside trials or prospective observational studies. This is especially true when a societal perspective is adopted, and patient non-medical costs (e.g., transportation, childcare, patient time involved in treatment) and use of over-the-counter medications and supplements are to be included.[39,47,73] In addition, administrative data are often not available, or would be burdensome to obtain for particular patient populations (e.g., the study enrolls patients across a number of clinic sites or who have a number of different health insurance plans), so self-report is also often required to capture healthcare utilization. When available, administrative data should be used to lower report burden, to avoid the problems of faulty memory recall, and to validate other patient reports.[47] However, most studies should plan to obtain at least some cost data directly from patients.

The two main methods used to obtain resource use from patients are cost diaries and cost questionnaires. Cost diaries are usually paper-and-pencil instruments sent home with patients (although they could be electronic or web-based reminders and data entry sites), with instructions that the patient record their healthcare utilization and other requested resource use as it occurs. These cost diaries are then collected by the study team at the end of each study-designated data collection period, and a new diary provided for use during the next period. Cost questionnaires are either self- or interviewer-administered instruments, requiring the patient to recall their resource use over the period of time since the last data collection point. Each method has its advantages and disadvantages. In general, cost diaries can provide more valid, complete and detailed information, but this benefit is offset by patient burden and noncompliance.[74,75] Cost questionnaires can have lower patient burden, but require patients to accurately recall their previous healthcare use.[47] It has also been suggested that studies utilize both methods together to improve data collection—i.e., give patients a cost diary to take home and record resource use as it occurs, and then ask (e.g., with a telephone or other reminder) that they have these cost diaries available as a reference when responding to the cost questionnaire.[47,74,76]

When cost diaries are used as data collection instruments (rather than just as reminders) they are usually distributed and collected weekly. However, if cost questionnaires are used, a decision is required as to the appropriate recall period—i.e., the maximum period between data collection points which will still generate valid data. A number of studies have addressed this issue, and it seems that the appropriate recall period depends to some extent on the data to be collected. Not surprisingly, patients are better at remembering more recent healthcare and other resource use.[74] They also have better recall for episodes that are more salient—e.g., longer hospital stays, visits for major illness, surgical versus non-surgical procedures—and worse recall (or at least reporting) for socially unacceptable or embarrassing events—e.g., testicular exams.[74] Obtaining data on medication use is especially challenging since it requires recall not only of the name of the medication, but also its strength, dosing, and duration of use. Of note for economic evaluations of CIM, it has been found that it is especially difficult for patients to accurately recall use of over-the-counter medications and supplements.[73,74,77] There is little evidence regarding recall of labs and diagnostic tests other than the fact that, in contrast to all other healthcare use, the tendency is for over- rather than under-estimation of use.[74] The shorter the recall period, the better. However, recall periods of one to six months have generally been considered acceptable.[19,74,75,78]

In most cases, each economic evaluation will need to design its own cost diary or cost questionnaire. In this design, some consideration should be given to the types and level of bundling of resources captured and reported in other published studies, and new instruments should be pre-tested for clarity.[76] Although a number of studies state that they used a cost diary or questionnaire of their own design, few publish the actual instrument. Goossens et al (2000) offers one example of a cost diary;[79] Mauskopf et al (1996) and Sherman et al (2001) contain examples of interviewer-administered cost questionnaires;[76,80] and Ritter et al (2001) and Gordon et al (2007) include examples of self-administered cost questionnaires.[78,81]

As is true for all data, data collected from patients on resource use and costs should have feasibility ranges specified and ongoing checks for completeness.[42,76] Since the analysis of the economic data will likely be performed by different analysts than that of the clinical data, the elements required for the economic analysis and their formatting should be pre-specified to make sure that complete data are transferred in a timely manner at study end.[42]

Published data

Data from published sources, including both the literature and publicly available databases, are usually only useful for economic evaluation via modeling. Although the methods involved in designing and building a mathematical model for economic evaluation are beyond the scope of this handbook, these data sources will be briefly reviewed here to demonstrate the scope of information available to such an enterprise.

Literature

The published literature is where any study should start. The design, outcomes measured, and results of similar previous trials, observational studies, or models can inform the design and outcomes to measure for any economic evaluation. However, modeling studies are especially dependent on the literature for estimates of the health effects of CIM and usual care. See Box 5 for an example of a CIM economic modeling study built entirely on estimates available in the literature.

Databases

The data available in published and/or publicly available databases can be used for a wide variety of estimates needed for modeling studies. These data can be used to estimate crucial model parameters such as the natural progression of a disease or healing (e.g., the probability that someone with acute low back pain will go on to chronic low back pain), and the healthcare resources typically used for various conditions (e.g., whether CIM is typically used alone for gastro-esophageal reflux, or in combination with conventional medication, or after conventional medication has failed).

A recent study by Lund and others[82] presents an extensive list of these data sources for the US. Below is a short list of those potentially most useful.

The American Time Use Survey (ATUS) – an annual, nationally representative survey of more than 26,000 Americans 15 or older from the Bureau of Labor Statistics. It provides estimates of the time patients (and their accompanying caregivers) spend on outpatient visits—useful data for the societal and patient perspectives.

The Medical Expenditure Panel Survey (MEPS) – an annual, nationally representative household survey by the Agency for Healthcare Quality and Research (AHRQ) of healthcare utilization and expenditures of 15,000 families and 35,000 individuals in the US. The household survey includes: demographic, income, health insurance, and employment characteristics; health conditions and health status; medical care resources used, charges and payments; and access to care and satisfaction with care. Advantages of MEPS data (as compared to claims datasets) are that this data source is well-known, considered of high quality, and includes expenditures from all providers (i.e., healthcare usage is not limited to services covered by insurance provider). Additionally, MEPS includes resource utilization and costs from uninsured individuals. Although the MEPS is a rich dataset, its disadvantages are that its information is limited to the most prevalent health conditions, and it is dependent upon self-report.

The National Health Interview Survey (NHIS) – a continuously administered survey by the Centers for Disease Control and Prevention (CDC) of 35,000 households containing about 87,500 persons in the US. The core component of the survey collects data on health status and limitations, injuries, healthcare access and utilization, health insurance, and income and assets. However, every few years the National Center for Complementary and Alternative Medicine (NCCAM) funds a supplement measuring the use of complementary therapies. The most recent of these surveys was 2007 and the next one is scheduled to be administered in 2012. There is also the possibility for connecting NHIS and MEPS data for the subset of MEPS patients who also completed the NHIS.

Medicare – publicly available data from Medicare make it a popular source healthcare utilization data. Datasets are comprised of representative samples and are downloaded for a fee (after a data use agreement is in place) from the Medicare website.

Expert opinion

This is the cost source of last resort. The use of expert opinion in an economic evaluation is generally frowned upon given the range of other data sources available. However, in older studies it was sometimes the only available option. If expert opinion is used (most often to estimate the cost of a particular bundle of procedures) it is important that the consensus of several reputable experts be obtained.

Productivity costs

It is appropriate to include the costs to the employer of gains or losses in productivity due to health in economic evaluations from the employer and societal perspectives. Note that even though this loss of productivity can also mean a loss of income to patients, lost productivity costs are not usually considered appropriate for inclusion in the patient perspective.[38] Instead, for the most part, the productivity loss costs included in economic evaluation are costs to employers, and thus, only apply to individuals who are employed. Losses of productive contributions by those outside the employment market are sometimes estimated and included in the societal perspective. However, these losses are still to those who benefit from this productivity and not to the individual.

Productivity costs can be large, and at times greater than direct medical costs, for many of the conditions treated by CIM—for example, low back pain, arthritis, anxiety and depression, asthma and migraine. [83-88] Therefore, these costs should be considered for inclusion in most economic evaluations of CIM, and in all using the societal perspective. Box 1 gives an example of a CIM economic evaluation where the inclusion of productivity costs had a substantial impact on the results.

There are two aspects of lost productivity to employers; absenteeism (absence from work) and presenteeism (reduced productivity while at work). Absenteeism data may be available from employer or other administrative sick leave or disability records. However, presenteeism is usually obtained through patient self-report.

There are several instruments available that capture presenteeism in a form which allows direct monetization.[89] Of these, one to consider is the Work Productivity and Activity Impairment (WPAI) Questionnaire. It is short (6 items), is easily modifiable to address the impact of any particular health issue or health in general, has been used most frequently in studies, has reasonable test-retest reliability and construct validity, and is in the public domain.[89-91] The WPAI captures absenteeism and presenteeism over the past week. Therefore, unless study data collection happens on a weekly basis, the WPAI's results should be treated as point estimates for productivity. In practice, this means that both presenteeism and absenteeism are assumed to change in a linear fashion between data collection points and that total change in productivity is captured using area-under-the-curve techniques net of baseline levels. It may also be useful to supplement the WPAI with a question on health-related absentee hours during the past data collection period. Evidence is limited, but it seems that recall periods of three to six months for absenteeism are acceptable and in general agreement with employer records of sick leave.[74]

For short-term absences (less than 2-6 months[92,93]) and for presenteeism, the human capital approach is used to value productivity loss. The human-capital approach values the hours lost to absenteeism and presenteeism at the employers' cost of employment (gross wages plus benefits and employment overhead).[26, p85] This is assumed to be the opportunity cost of production to the employer, since this is how much the employer pays for a productive worker's time. For longer absences, or when worker productivity is lost due to premature death, it has been argued that a friction-cost approach is more appropriate.[92,93] Under this approach, it is assumed that at some point (i.e., after the "friction period") the employer will replace the worker. Therefore, the costs of productivity losses to the employer are the lost hours of production during the friction period, plus the cost of recruiting and training a replacement worker.[38]

Most CIM interventions address conditions which affect short-term absence and presenteeism. Therefore, in most cases the human-capital approach will be appropriate. However, because some short-term productivity losses may be made up by the employee upon return to work (or by colleagues), and because the work not made up may consist of a worker's less important tasks, productivity losses should be reported separately and considered in sensitivity analyses.[26]

Unit costs

The best way to estimate costs is to measure resource use and then apply a unit cost. Unit costs should be consistent with the units used for measuring resource use (e.g., a cost per visit for outpatient visits), the study's perspective (e.g., the cost of a visit to the payer is different than to the patient), and its time horizon (i.e., unit costs should all reflect the same currency year).[42] Some data sources (especially administrative data such as claims) contain information on both resource use and unit costs. For other sources, such as self-report, the data on resource use will need to have an exogenous unit cost applied to estimate costs. Even when actual unit cost data (such as actual employer costs of wages and benefits) are available, such as from a trial, it is often more appropriate for the societal perspective and transferability if statewide, regional or national estimates are used.[42]

Unit costs can be obtained from a variety of published sources, and it is recommended that study documentation include a list of the unit cost used for each resource and its source. Some general sources include the *Drug Topics Red Book* which contains average wholesale prices (AWPs) for prescription and over-the-counter drugs; Drugstore.com which provides retail prices for drugs, including over-the-counter medications and some supplements; and various Centers for Medicare & Medicaid Services (CMS) reports on the cost of physician visits and hospital stays.[94] These CMS reports are sources for usual Medicare reimbursements—"the de facto national standard price schedules" for the US.[34, p81] When gathering unit cost data, remember that the ideal unit cost is the opportunity cost of the resource, and that is usually closer to the allowed *cost* of a health plan, for example, than the provider's *charges*.[72] Charges are generally larger than costs, and are designed to try to make up for expenses not covered by payments from large health plans with deeply discounted rates.

In each case, the currency year used should be determined (e.g., costs reported in 2008 US dollars) and unit costs from different years should be adjusted so that all reflect the study's currency year (usually the year that represents the bulk of the healthcare utilization data) by using the appropriate consumer price index (such as the medical care components of the CPI, published by the US Bureau of Labor Statistics, or the health-related components of the European Central Bank's Harmonized Index of Consumer Prices). Due to dramatic cost structure differences across countries, it is rarely suitable to use unit costs from another country, even if an appropriate exchange rate is applied. It is usual that caregiver, volunteer, and other non-paid time be valued at an average hourly wage rate.[35,39]

Unfortunately, unit costs for most CIM therapies are not generally available in the literature. Therefore, micro-costing, a survey of practitioners, or contact with a national association might be required to generate an appropriate unit cost. Uncertainty in this estimate, as well as in other unit costs, can be addressed in the sensitivity analysis.

Chapter 6. Measurement of health outcomes

Economic evaluations in healthcare compare costs to health benefits. The previous chapter discussed costs. This chapter addresses the issues specific to the measurement of health outcomes.

Which health benefits should be measured

The type of economic evaluation is determined by the health benefits used in the study.

Cost-effectiveness analysis (CEA)

If a CEA is planned then health benefits should be measured in some natural commonly-used unit for the disease category or condition of interest. For example, for cardiovascular disease (CVD) risk reduction, a common unit is years of life gained. Theoretically, if all economic studies of therapies for a particular disease category report their results in terms of cost per some common unit, then the costs can be directly compared across studies and alternatives. Therefore, it is important to review the literature to ensure that you are measuring health benefits using at least one of the common units. Note that you can measure health benefits and report cost-effectiveness in terms of more than one type of health outcome.

A review of the CEA literature for diabetes, CVD, hypertension, and dyslipidemia indicates that most use life-years saved as their health outcome. However, some report cost effectiveness in terms of other outcomes. Examples include costs per case of diabetes prevented,[95] cost per additional patient with good control of hypertension,[96] cost per cardiovascular event avoided,[97] cost per additional day free of depression,[98] cost per mmol/L decrease in serum low-density lipoprotein,[99] cost per cardiovascular complication averted,[100] cost per pound of weight lost,[99] and cost per mmol/L decrease in blood glucose.[99]

Cost-utility analysis (CUA)

If a CUA is planned then a measure of "utility" is needed. The term utility is used in health economics as a quantitative indicator of individuals' preferences for one health state over another. Utility measures attempt to combine the broad health-related quality of life impacts and the length of life impacts of a therapy. The benefit of using a utility measure is that it is applicable to all patients and diseases, creating a level playing field across programs. Ideally, by using this measure of health benefits, therapies such as those targeting diabetes can be directly compared to therapies targeting other conditions such as low back pain, in terms of both their cost and overall impact on health. There are several utility (and utility-like) measures available (e.g., disability-adjusted life-years or DALYs and quality-adjusted life-expectancy or QALEs), but the one most commonly used is the quality-adjusted life-year (QALY). One QALY equals one full year at perfect health. Half a QALY equals either one full year at a health-related quality of life of 0.5 (half way between perfect health, which is 1.0, and dead, which is zero) or, equivalently, half a year at perfect health.

There are two main approaches to the measurement of QALYs. One is to measure them directly from study participants using methods such as rating, standard gamble, or time trade-off techniques.[101] These methods elicit the preferences of individuals in the study sample as to the relative value they place on various health states. These methods have several disadvantages; thus, are rarely used.[42,44,102] They require respondents to consider their own death. They are often not sensitive to clinically significant changes in health, and are subject to random variation (i.e., they lack reliability). They take considerable time and study resources to do correctly. And the results reflect the preferences of the study sample, rather than society as a whole. To this last point, the U.S Panel on Cost-Effectiveness in Health and Medicine in their definition of the "reference case" (which is intended for use in resource allocation) suggests the use of population preferences to define the QALYs used in cost-utility analysis from the societal perspective.[13] However, it may be appropriate to consider collecting preferences for health states (utilities) directly from the patients themselves for use in the patient's perspective.

The second main approach to QALYs involves the measurement of health states (and changes in these states) from the study sample, and then the application of preference (utility) weights to these health states. The three main instruments for which societal preference weights are available are the EuroQol EQ-5D, the Health Utilities Index (HUI), and the SF-6D. The EQ-5D[103] is a five-item instrument which has preference weights available based on representative samples of the US[104] and UK[105] populations, as well as for a number of other countries. The use of the EQ-5D results in a five-number score for the health state of each patient comprised of a number between 1 and 3 (1=best; 3=worse) for each of the five dimensions of health measured (mobility, self-care, usual activities, pain/discomfort, anxiety/depression). Registration is required for use of the EQ-5D and fees may apply.

The HUI[106] is proprietary and comes in two versions: the HUI2 (seven attributes each with 3-5 levels; originally designed for childhood cancer patients) and the newer HUI3 (eight attributes each with 5-6 levels; designed for a general population). Preference/utility weights are applied using a scoring algorithm based on a large community sample in Canada.

The third measure, commonly used in economic evaluations of CIM, is the SF-6D. This measure uses a subset of items from either the SF-36[107] or SF-12[108] instruments and an algorithm estimated from a UK sample to calculate QALYs. A signed license agreement with QualityMetric is required for the use of the SF-36 or SF-12 instruments. The SF-36 algorithm[107] can also be used with the RAND-36 which is available online without cost or restriction.

Most economic evaluations of CIM use either (or both) the EQ-5D or the SF-6D. One consideration in choosing between the two is that the EQ-5D has been shown to have ceiling effects and the SF-6D to have floor effects.[109] It may be that the HUI3 also has ceiling effects,[110] but they may not be as limiting as seen in the EQ-5D.[111] As a result the EQ-5D or HUI3 may be more sensitive to changes in health for populations with severe health deficiencies, and for otherwise generally well populations (the populations often targeted by CIM) the SF-6D may be more sensitive.

Cost-benefit analysis (CBA)

If a CBA is planned then the study must measure some unit of health which is then given a monetary value. As previously discussed, putting a monetary value on health and life is controversial. In general, one of three techniques is used: human capital, revealed preferences, and stated preferences of "willingness to pay" (WTP), which use survey methods such as contingent valuation.[26, p215] The human capital approach values health in terms of renewed or increased productivity valued at the market wage rate. Thus, a measure of productivity is required. Problems with this approach include the appropriate wage rate to use, the fact that the health benefits of higher wage earners would be given a higher value than the health benefits of those earning lower wages (or who are unemployed), and the difficulty of valuing time not spent in the workplace. Because of these issues, this method may not be appropriate for evaluations from the societal perspective, especially when targeting health effects other than those captured by work productivity (e.g., well-being). However, this approach may be very appropriate for a CBA from the employer's perspective. One survey of CBAs in healthcare found that most (70%) used the human capital approach to value health benefits.[25]

Revealed preference techniques rely on studies of actual choices made to value health. The two main types that have been used are studies of the amount of additional money workers demand to take on jobs with higher health risks, and studies of the compensation awarded by judges to victims whose health has been damaged. Both approaches have serious problems (i.e., other influences on wages in the first, and the vagaries of the tort system in the second); thus, revealed preference approaches have not been used much in practice. The above-mentioned survey of CBAs in healthcare only found one study that used court awards as its estimate of the value of health.[25]

Various survey techniques (generally called contingent valuation or stated preference surveys) are used to elicit willingness to pay (WTP). Contingent valuation is most often used in consumer product design and marketing (to determine consumers' likely demand for new products) and in environmental economics (to value resources such as clean air and water, and open space). The most basic method to elicit WTP is through an open-ended survey question—e.g., how much would you have paid to achieve the health benefits you received? Examples of WTP elicitation in CIM include a study of the use of CIM for allergies where CIM users were asked how much they would pay for the health benefits they achieved. Just over half would pay more than what they had paid in out-of-pocket costs, and just over another quarter said that the health benefits were worth about what they paid. Unfortunately, the non-CIM users were not asked the same question.[112]

More sophisticated contingent valuation methods (e.g., conjoint analysis or discrete choice experiments) ask respondents about hypothetical scenarios regarding the health issue under consideration. Conjoint analysis is a technique that asks respondents to make tradeoffs among attributes (i.e., characteristics) and attribute levels to determine preferences for alternative products (e.g., packages of care) and/or outcomes. This approach is being used more often in healthcare and, if cost is included as an attribute, can be used to elicit WTP.[113] Conjoint analysis is of special interest in CIM because it allows for the valuation of benefits beyond health,[15] such as process utility.[114] For example, a study of patient preferences for homeopathic and conventional treatment for asthma used conjoint analysis to determine the relative importance to patients of the extent to which the doctor took time to listen and treated them as a whole person in addition to the effectiveness of the treatment.[115] Unfortunately, cost wasn't explicitly included in the attributes considered, and these respondents were queried about what was important about the care they were already receiving (rather than choosing across possible combinations of care and outcome attributes). However, these types of studies have the potential to determine the relative importance and monetary value patients put on both the process of care and its outcomes.

Contingent valuation is being used more often in healthcare to determine willingness to pay. However, the application of these methods requires additional data collection effort; the results are affected by individuals' ability to pay and suffer from both over- and under-estimation when compared to revealed preference; and the technique requires care when used in CBA to avoid double-counting (respondents need to separately value health from other sources of already-counted costs).[26,116]

Cost consequence analysis (CCA)

A CCA allows decision makers to select the components of costs and health benefits most relevant to their perspective and needs.[17,26,117] Basically, instead of (or in addition to) reporting an incremental CEA or CUA ratio, the economic evaluation reports estimates for each cost component (e.g., direct outpatient visit costs, medication costs, participant travel costs, indirect/productivity costs, etc.) and for each health effect (e.g., improvement in each biomarker, stress reduction, increase in self-efficacy, changes in quality of life, absentee days reduced, QALY gains, etc.) for each arm of the study. This approach is important for CIM for two reasons. First, it allows measurement and acknowledgment of a full range of health (and non-health) impacts seen in CIM.[118] Second, and more generally, it is believed that this method of reporting outcomes may improve decision makers' use of economic information.[117]

Table 4 gives the format for a hypothetical example of a cost-consequence analysis (CCA) for a healing-oriented CIM practice. CCA results can be reported all in one table as shown in this example, or in two or more tables as needed. The list of health outcomes shown here is one example from a variety of possibilities. Since most CIM therapies treat the whole person, they tend to have broad impacts—often extending beyond health. Outcomes can include improvements in function, energy, mood, learning ability, and harder-to-measure, but no less important, consequences such as creativity, innovation, compassion, and altruism. One of the benefits of the CCA format is that it allows recognition and inclusion of all measureable outcomes.

Table 4. Example cost-consequence analysis table format for a hypothetical study of CIM-related classes for low back pain

	Treatment Mean (SD)	Control Mean (SD)	Difference (95% CI)
Health outcomes			
Back pain-related dysfunction			
Characteristic pain intensity			
Bothersomeness of back pain			
Depression			
Anxiety			
Global health improvement			
Mindfulness			
Pain acceptance			
Pain beliefs/appraisals			
Pain coping strategies			
Overall mental health			
Overall physical health			
Quality-adjusted life years (QALYs)			
Patient satisfaction			

Costs and Economic Outcomes					
	Units Mean (95% CI)	Costs (95% CI)	Units Mean (95% CI)	Costs (95% CI)	Difference (95% CI)
Direct medical costs					
Intervention (classes)					
Medications					
Outpatient visits					
Specialist visits					
ER visits					
Hospitalizations					
Direct non-medical costs					
Patient treatment time					
Transportation costs					
Childcare costs					
Indirect costs					
Absenteeism					
Presenteeism					

95% CI = 95% confidence interval; those calculated for costs (and other non-normal data) should be calculated using bias-corrected and accelerated bootstrap techniques

Approaches similar to the Outcomes Tree[119] or the Framework for Outcome Domains[120] can be used to help identify the full range of outcomes to include. These approaches use a bio-psychosocial framework to organize the potential outcomes of CIM into domains (e.g., social, psychological, physical, spiritual, behavioral, biological, etc.). Specific outcomes are then selected from each of the relevant domains for analysis. This approach can provide decision makers with a more "holistic" view of the range of impacts possible from practices that are thought to induce whole-person healing processes. Of course, valid measures, appropriate for the therapy under study, must be selected, and for cross-study comparability, at least one should also be used in other published studies targeting the condition of interest. One source for a variety of outcome measures is the online outcomes database hosted by IN-CAM, a complementary and alternative medicine research network.[120]

How health benefits are measured

There has been much written on the challenges of measuring the health impacts of CIM.[121-124] Because full economic evaluations require estimates of both costs and health impacts, these challenges will also apply to economic evaluations of CIM.

A related point is that the measure of health effects required for economic evaluation is one which could be expected from the therapy in a real world setting. Therefore, the health effects of a therapy should be measured in a pragmatic (effectiveness) trial or an observational study, or obtained from an appropriately designed systematic review (i.e., one that focuses only on the results of effectiveness trials or appropriately adjusts efficacy trial results). Health effects measured in tightly controlled studies (e.g., randomized double-blind placebo-controlled trials; aka efficacy or explanatory trials) are not likely replicable in the real world (i.e., tend to have low external validity), and therefore are inappropriate for use in an economic evaluation. A good effectiveness trial balances between internal validity (i.e., can I believe these results in this sample?) and external validity (i.e., can I believe these results will also occur elsewhere?) and is a good source of health effect estimates for economic evaluation.[49,50,125,126]

CHAPTER 7. STATISTICAL ANALYSIS

One of the most surprising things about economic evaluation to those accustomed to analyzing clinical trial data is that it does not (necessarily) require sophisticated statistical software. Almost all of what is needed for a basic analysis can be done in a spreadsheet program. It is a simple comparison of benefits to costs, after all. That being said, the analysis required to get to that simple comparison can be quite detailed, sophisticated and involved. The analysis involved in an economic evaluation includes many of the same techniques that are used in clinical trials (if the evaluation is alongside a clinical trial), in epidemiological studies (if the evaluation uses observational data) and in meta-analysis (if the evaluation uses modeling). However, the analysis then goes beyond these techniques to require attention to the time value of outcomes (for studies that measure impacts past one year), non-parametric methods (because cost data rarely follow a normal distribution), and a broader analysis of uncertainty (sample variance plus the impact of assumptions).

The basic analysis

Before getting into the details, let's start with the most satisfying part of the analysis: the end, where all the hard work comes together to give an answer. Table 5 shows the basic equations for the main types of economic evaluation: CBA, CEA, and CUA. Cost-consequence analysis (CCA) skips this step, and instead simply lists all the possible inputs to these equations. When applying these equations there are a couple of things to note. First, the differences in costs and effects are usually calculated as the new therapy under consideration (e.g., the CIM therapy) minus the status quo (e.g., usual care). This is because we are looking at the changes that would happen if we adopted the new therapy. Second, the health effects are always thought of as health improvements. So, if you have a measure where a decrease is considered an improvement in health, as in the next example, the negative of the difference is reported. That is, the incremental health improvement is reported.

Table 5. Basic equations for the main types of full economic evaluation

	Cost-benefit analysis (CBA)	Cost-effectiveness analysis (CEA)	Cost-utility analysis (CUA) (a special case of CEA)
Unit of health outcome	Monetary units (e.g., US dollars)	Natural units (e.g., percentage points of glycosylated hemoglobin or HbA1c)	Units of overall impact on length and quality of life (e.g., quality-adjusted life-years, QALY)
Results	Net benefits $(B_2-B_1) - (C_2-C_1-S_2+S_1)$	Incremental cost-effectiveness ratio* $(C_2-C_1-S_2+S_1)/(E_2-E_1)$	Incremental cost-utility ratio* $(C_2-C_1-S_2+S_1)/(QALY_2-QALY_1)$

B_1 = monetary value of gains in health from alternative 1 (often usual care); B_2 = monetary value of the gains in health from alternative 2 (the new therapy); C_1 = total input costs of alternative 1; C_2 = total input costs of alternative 2; S_1 = total cost savings (economic outcomes) for alternative 1; S_2 = total cost savings (economic outcomes) for alternative 2; E_1 = health gains from alternative 1; E_2 = health gains from alternative 2; $QALY_1$ = quality-adjusted life-years gained from alternative 1; $QALY_2$ = quality-adjusted life-years gained from alternative 2.

* Ratios are calculated when both the costs and the effects (positive health outcomes) of one therapy are higher than those of another. When the costs are lower and the effects are higher for one therapy, it is said to dominate the alternative (and the alternative is said to be dominated) and no ratio is presented.

Table 6 contains examples of CEAs of CIM. The first three columns show the results of a study comparing the Alexander technique (a set of six training sessions to develop lifelong skills for postural awareness self-care) to normal care for back pain.[15,127] The second three columns contain results from a study of adjunctive preoperative oral supplementation (arginine and omega-3 fatty acids) for patients undergoing surgery for gastrointestinal cancer.[128] The health effects for the back pain study are measured in terms of a Roland-Morris disability score, a scale where a higher number indicates worse health. Therefore, when the difference is taken between the results of the Alexander technique (a Roland-Morris score of 6.7) and normal care (a Roland-Morris score of 8.1) even though the mathematical difference is -1.4 (a reduction in the worsening of health), it is reported as 1.4 (the health improvement). The health effects of the surgery study are reported as the percent of patients who did not experience surgical complications. Here a higher number indicates better health, so the sign of the difference is straightforward (50.0 − 62.8 = 12.8). The costs for the back pain study use the UK's National Health Service perspective and the costs for the surgery study use the hospital's perspective. In both cases the savings (S) have already been subtracted from the up-front costs (C) for each therapy.

Table 6. Examples of the final cost-effectiveness analysis calculations for two CIM studies

	For chronic or recurrent back pain*			For patients undergoing surgery for gastrointestinal cancer†		
	Normal care$_1$	Alexander technique $_2$	Difference (2 − 1)	Conven-tional care$_1$	Supple-mentation$_2$	Difference (2 − 1)
Costs (C − S)	£54	£218	£163	€3122	€1872	-€1250
Effects (E)‡	8.1	6.7	1.4	50.0%	62.8%	12.8%
Increm ental cost-effectiv eness ratio (ICER)			£113/RMD point reduced			Supple-mentation domin-ates

* Taken from Table 4 of Little et al (2008)[127] and Tables 4 and 5 in Hollinghurst et al (2008)[129]

† Taken from Table 7 in Braga et al (2005)[128]

‡ The health effects in the back pain study are points on the Roland-Morris disability scale with lower values indicating better health. The health effects for the surgery study are measured as the percent of patients who do not experience complications from surgery.

RMD = Roland-Morris disability score

Following the equation shown in Table 5 for CEA, recognizing that savings have already been subtracted from input costs, and acknowledging the need to correct the sign for the health effects (as discussed above), we get (£218 - £54)/-(6.7 − 8.1) which is £163/1.4 or £113 per reduced point on the Roland-Morris disability score for the back pain study. This amount may or may not be considered cost-effective. It depends on whether this reduction in disability is worth £113 to the National Health Service.

In the case of the surgery study, the calculation of a ratio is inappropriate. This is because one of the components of the ratio (in this case incremental cost increase) is negative—i.e., the intervention is cost saving. The creation and reporting of a ratio in this case would result in a negative ratio, and the loss of information as to whether the cause was cost savings (negative cost increases) or a loss in health (negative health gains). Therefore, the therapy with the better costs and health effects, in this case the addition of supplementation, is said to dominate in comparison to conventional care alone. Equivalently, the conventional care option can be said to be dominated.

Timeframe and discounting

The next step out from the basic analysis above involves the concept of discounting. Discounting is only applicable if the timeframe of the economic evaluation is longer than one year.

The appropriate timeframe for an economic evaluation is a period long enough to capture the main health effects and cost impacts of the therapy under consideration. Of course, because longer studies tend to be more expensive to run, the choice of a study timeframe also needs to be balanced against the available budget. Choosing the appropriate timeframe for studies of CIM is especially challenging. Because CIM therapies tend to have a large prevention component, time is required to show effects and generate cost savings. On the other hand, research funding for CIM is scarce, often making longer-term studies infeasible. Economic modeling can be used as an alternative to a clinical trial or as a way to estimate a therapy's longer-term impacts.

If the study period is longer than one year, both the costs and health effects that occur past the first year must be discounted. This is primarily due to the existence of time preference.[26, p38] Time preference refers to the fact that we, individually and collectively, prefer to have dollars, resources, or health improvements now, as opposed to later, because we can benefit from each of these in the interim. The goal is to adjust all costs and effects to reflect their value at the point in time when the result of the decision under consideration would go into place—the real or hypothetical date at which the new therapy would be implemented. Therefore, costs and health effects that would occur far in the future in relation to that time point (conventionally, more than one year from that decision point) must be adjusted to be comparable to the more immediate cost and health effects.

The basic equation to discount either costs or health effects (each over n years) is:

$$PV = X_1/(1+dr)^0 + X_2/(1+dr)^1 + X_3/(1+dr)^2 + X_4/(1+dr)^3 + ... + X_n/(1+dr)^{(n-1)}$$

Where:

   PV = the present value of the stream of costs or health effects

   X = the cost or health effects seen in year n

   dr = the discount rate

Costs and health effects should be discounted separately. The present value of each stream is the amount entered as a B, C, E, S, or QALY in Table 5. Note that it is important to report the year to which the costs and health effects are discounted—i.e., the year of the decision point—and this year is also the currency year used for costs.

The appropriate discount rate depends on the perspective of the analysis and whether the future costs are estimated (or measured) in constant or nominal dollars. If the same unit cost numbers are applied to resources used or saved over all these years, the dollar amounts are then in constant dollars. If instead, unit costs are adjusted for inflation over years, or if actual costs are used each year, the amounts are in nominal dollars. For constant dollars, a "real" discount rate is used, which is one that does not include inflation. A real discount rate is also used to discount health effects as they are not affected by inflation. For nominal dollars, a nominal discount rate is used. If inflation is positive (i.e., it is not a period of deflation) then the nominal discount rate will be higher than the real discount rate.

The appropriate discount rate also depends on the perspective used for the evaluation. This is because the time preference for dollars, resources, and health are different if you approach it from the point of view of an individual patient versus the point of view of society as a whole. The value of time preference comes from what you could do with the dollars, resources or health effects in the interim between now and having them in the future. Individuals tend to have more options and thus put more value on this interim period than does society as a whole. Thus, the discount rate to use for individuals is usually the highest, the rate for society the lowest, and the rates for a hospital, health plan or employer lie in between.

Choosing a discount rate is the stuff of dissertations and careers. However, there are two sources of assistance. First, various government and regulatory agencies have made recommendations as to the appropriate discount rate to use for the societal perspective. The US Panel on Cost-

Effectiveness in Health and Medicine recommends the use of a real annual discount rate of 3% in their reference case—i.e., CUA from the societal perspective. [13, p233] Second, no matter the discount rate chosen, its effect on results can be (and are recommended to be) tested in sensitivity analyses. For more detail on discount rates see Chapter 7 of Gold et al (1996) Cost-Effectiveness in Health and Medicine.[13]

Handling missing data

Missing data are a challenge for all research, but because an economic evaluation depends on the repeated measurement of a number of variables in order to capture costs, it is especially problematic for economic evaluations alongside clinical trials.

The handling of missing data is directly related to the concept of "intent to treat" (ITT). ITT is an analysis strategy of randomized pragmatic trials that compares patients in the groups to which they were originally randomly assigned.[130] It is recommended that economic evaluations alongside clinical trials follow this strategy.[42] This is generally interpreted as including all patients who were randomized, regardless of whether it turned out that they satisfied the eligibility criteria, the treatment actually received, or subsequent withdrawal or deviation from protocol. There are two main purposes of using ITT. First, it preserves the similarity across groups supposedly created by randomization. Second, it allows for non-compliance and deviations from protocol, such as would be expected in actual practice. Complete case analysis (only including subjects with complete data) generally violates the ITT principle. Thus efforts to ensure complete follow-up are the best answer, and the proper treatment of missing data is the next best alternative.

There are two main types of methods to address missing data: naïve and principled.[131,132] Naïve methods estimate (impute) a single value with which to fill in each missing data point. This use of a single value biases estimates of variance for the dataset as a whole (thus, biases confidence intervals and p-values), because the imputed value is treated as known. Principled methods (aka multiple imputation methods) impute a range of values with which to fill in each missing data point, resulting in a number of different versions of the full dataset. Analyses are then performed on each version of the dataset and the results pooled allowing for the uncertainty in the imputations to be appropriately reflected in the analysis.

The method to use for missing data depends on the reason the data are missing, and the proper treatment of missing data has been the topic of numerous articles and books.[131-134] However, in economic evaluation the use of a multiple imputation approach is recommended in the majority of cases.[42,133] For a good book on the topic try McKnight et al. *Missing Data: A Gentle Introduction*[134] (as a caution, one typo has been identified in this book on page 204 in a key equation; the third line should say "the five *squared* standard errors").

In summary, use of the intent to treat strategy or principle, which is recommended for the analysis of pragmatic trial data, incorporates the need to include individuals who are lost to follow-up. This requires minimizing loss to follow-up, and appropriately dealing with missing data when it occurs. No matter the approach taken, the prevalence of missing data, and the method(s) used to address them should be reported in the economic evaluation. In addition, the effectiveness of the missing data imputation technique should be addressed in the evaluation's sensitivity analysis.

Confidence intervals via bootstrapping

Cost data from clinical trials are notoriously skewed. There is usually a large portion of a sample with no (or small) costs and a few with extremely high costs, such as from unexpected hospitalization. In response to this determined non-normality, many statisticians have resorted to transforming the data, reporting medians, excluding outliers, and using non-parametric tests.

When information about the costs of alternative therapies is needed to guide health policy, it is the total budget for the target population that is important. To get this number, a healthcare planner multiplies the number of patients in that population by the average cost per patient. Therefore, it is the mean (the arithmetic average) value for costs that should be reported.[70,135-137] The difference between two means is usually evaluated using a t-test. However, the t-test relies on an assumption of normality in the underlying data. Various methods have been used to enable a comparison of means in highly skewed data. The approach most often recommended is the bias-corrected and accelerated (BCa) non-parametric bootstrap method of generating confidence intervals.[135-137] This method not only allows confidence intervals for cost data, but also can be used to illustrate the uncertainty around the point estimate for the incremental cost-effectiveness ratio (ICER).

Bootstrapping is a technique that draws a number of samples with replacement from the original trial sample for each group. These resamples each contain the same number of subjects as the original trial sample. But since the samples are drawn with replacement, certain subjects will be included more than once in some resamples and will be left out of other resamples. Simulation studies have shown that 1000 replications (drawn resamples which are then analyzed) are sufficient for stable estimates.[138] There are several software programs available to generate BCa bootstrap estimates, but these estimates can also be generated using formulas built into a standard spreadsheet program. The estimates of incremental costs and incremental effects for each of the 1000 bootstrap replications are often graphed as a scatter plot showing the variation around the ICER point estimate on a cost-effectiveness plane.[26] A good book on bootstrapping is the classic 1993 monograph by Bradley Efron and Robert Tibshirani, *An Introduction to the Bootstrap*.[139]

Figure 3 gives an example of the results of a hypothetical economic evaluation plotted on a cost-effectiveness plane. In this example, the hypothetical treatment generated an average of 0.02 additional QALYs at an average cost savings of $638 per participant. The scatter of the bootstrap replications illustrates the sample variation around those estimates. On this graph, 72 percent of the cost-utility pairs are cost saving and improve health.

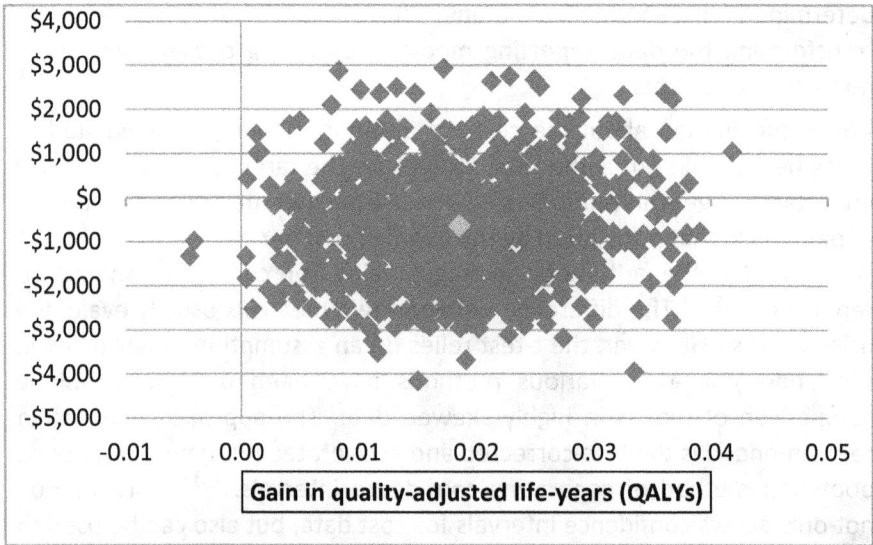

Figure 3. Bootstrapped cost-utility pairs graphed on a cost-effectiveness plane

Sensitivity analysis

Uncertainty in an economic evaluation comes not just from sample variation, but from imputation-related uncertainty and other assumptions made, such as unit costs and the discount rate.[42,140] Sampling uncertainty comes from the variability of the population under study in a clinical trial. This variation is addressed through the presentation of confidence intervals and graphing of the incremental cost and incremental effectiveness pairs generated by bootstrapping (Figure 3).[26] Results for CUAs can also be presented as a cost-effectiveness acceptability curve, which provides a graphical depiction of the probability that the therapy of interest is cost-effective against various threshold values of societal willingness-to-pay for a QALY gained.[47,141] Figure 4 shows a cost-effectiveness acceptability curve for the same hypothetical economic evaluation depicted in Figure 3.

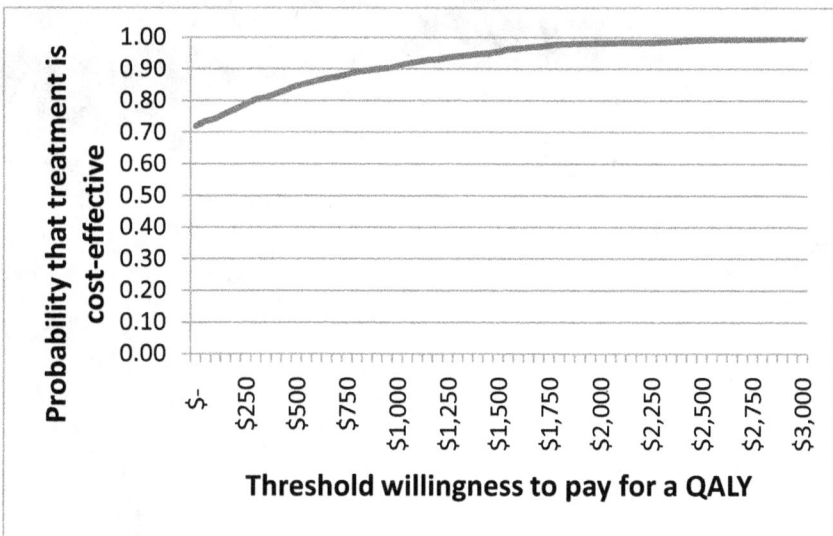

Figure 4. Cost-effectiveness acceptability curve

The other sources of uncertainty are usually addressed through univariate or probabilistic sensitivity analyses. These analyses test the robustness of study results to the data imputation method and to various study assumptions by varying one assumption at a time (univariate) or by allowing all to vary (probabilistic). Usually data imputation is tested by comparing study results to the results that would have been generated under complete case analysis or under other imputation methods. Common study assumptions which should each be subjected to sensitivity analysis include unit costs (if they come from any source other than the trial itself, and especially those used for non-market items such as volunteer or caregiver time), whether disease-specific only or all economic outcomes are included, how productivity losses are estimated and valued, the discount rate used (if the study is longer than one year), and any study assumption that could have a substantial impact on study outcomes. Modeling studies are full of assumptions requiring sensitivity analysis.

Chapter 8. Interpreting and Reporting the Results of Economic Evaluations of CIM

Proper interpretation and reporting of economic evaluations are important for a number of reasons. These include ensuring that the results are accessible and useful to targeted (and potential) decision makers, making the results as potentially transferable to other settings as possible, and getting the study published.

Guidelines for the publication of economic evaluations

There have been several different sets of guidelines published regarding the quality of economic evaluations.[142-146] The *BMJ* has published a guideline for their economic submissions,[147] and this or another of the published checklists should be followed for all economic evaluation manuscripts. These guidelines are to economic evaluations what the various CONSORT statements are to manuscripts describing the results of clinical trials. To this end, note that the proper write-up of an economic evaluation requires its own manuscript; separate from the one reporting effectiveness results, if the economic evaluation was performed alongside a clinical trial. It is recommended that one or more of these guidelines be obtained early in the study design process so that study authors are prepared to respond to the information required in their manuscript. Examples of well-reported economic evaluations of CIM, in terms of the BMJ checklist, include:

- Wonderling et al (2004)[148] – a study of acupuncture for chronic headache.
- Hollinghurst et al (2008)[129]- a study of Alexander technique and massage for low back pain.
- Herman et al (2008)[27] – a study of naturopathic care for chronic low back pain.

Interpretation of the results of economic evaluations

There are four main outcomes from an economic evaluation and these each relate to a quadrant of what has been called a cost-effectiveness decision matrix (Figure 5).

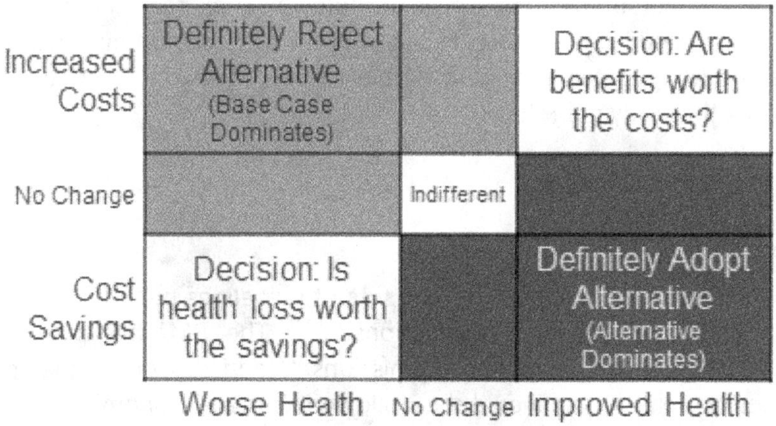

Increased Costs	Definitely Reject Alternative (Base Case Dominates)		Decision: Are benefits worth the costs?
No Change		Indifferent	
Cost Savings	Decision: Is health loss worth the savings?		Definitely Adopt Alternative (Alternative Dominates)
	Worse Health	No Change	Improved Health

Figure 5. Cost-effectiveness decision matrix

The horizontal dimension of this matrix is determined by the results of effectiveness trials and captures the answer to the question of whether the therapy under consideration provides better or worse health outcomes than usual care. Clearly, in most cases, a decision maker would give more positive consideration to a therapy that improves health outcomes—i.e., has results which land on the right side of the matrix. The vertical dimension is determined by costs and is the dimension added by economic evaluation. Here, in most cases, a decision maker would give more positive consideration to a therapy that reduces costs (as compared to usual care), so preference would be given to results landing in the lower part of this matrix.

If a therapy both improves health outcomes and lowers costs compared to usual care (i.e., lands in the lower-right quadrant), then that therapy is said to dominate, and the message from the economic evaluation would be that this therapy should be strongly considered for adoption. Of course, there are other considerations that must be taken into account (including equity, ethics, and legal issues) in the final decision. If health is improved, but at a cost, be cautious about declaring something as cost-effective. Remember that whether something is or is not cost-effective is a judgment call that is ultimately up to the decision maker,[149] and the resources to implement a higher-cost effective therapy (i.e., therapies in the top-right quadrant of the matrix) have to come from somewhere.

Generalization of the results of economic evaluations

Whereas health outcomes are, to some extent, considered generalizable across settings, economic outcomes are usually not.[6] This is because human physiology and psychology are generally more consistent and replicable across settings than are resource availability, practice patterns, the expertise of staff, financial incentives to providers and local prices.[59] Basically, "[o]perational efficiency may not be relevant to the clinical outcome, but it is critical to the cost outcome."[59, p695] Therefore, whereas meta-analysis can be used across the results of a number of trials to generate broad (i.e., generalizable) statements regarding the efficacy (or effectiveness) of a particular therapy for a particular health condition, similar broad statements regarding cost-effectiveness are usually not possible. The results of any particular study should be reported as specific to that setting—i.e., "the addition of individualized acupuncture provided by Traditional Chinese Medicine-trained, licensed acupuncturists practicing in private acupuncture clinics in the UK for low back pain is cost saving from the societal perspective when compared to usual care alone."[32]

One goal in economic evaluation is to ensure the *transferability* of study results—i.e., to provide enough study detail so that results can be adapted (usually via modeling) to apply to other settings.[7] See Box 5 for an example of the use of modeling to adapt study results from other settings. Studies have shown that the aspect of setting which has the most effect on costs is unit price.[150] Fortunately, the problem of price variation across settings is the easiest to handle methodologically, through the separate reporting of resource use and unit costs.[11,45] Therefore, economic evaluations of CIM should at least meet this reporting requirement.

Final points

Complementary and integrative medicine (CIM) is usually defined as those approaches to health that are outside mainstream medicine.[8] In overcoming this exclusion, CIM faces a number of challenges of credibility as well as the need to show safety, effectiveness, and cost-effectiveness. Therefore, effectiveness trials and economic evaluations of CIM may have to meet a higher quality bar than those of conventional medicine. There is also limited funding for all research, but especially for CIM. This is why well-designed and well-done effectiveness trials are essential, and economic evaluations should be added wherever possible. It is also imperative that the results of these efforts be well-reported. It is only by generating high-quality evidence that CIM can be considered at the healthcare policy table.

RESOURCES

The following resources are recommended for those interested in more detail on economic evaluation in general, and are especially recommended for those considering undertaking an economic evaluation of CIM. In addition to these, note the references cited and recommended readings in various parts of this handbook.

Generally acknowledged as the best reference on economic evaluation in healthcare; make sure to get the latest edition:

> Drummond MF, Sculpher MJ, Torrance GW, O'Brien BJ, Stoddart GL. *Methods for the Economic Evaluation of Health Care Programmes*. Third Edition ed. Oxford: Oxford University Press, 2005.

There are a number of different resources available for economic modeling. This is a good one and the authors are all recognized as experts in the economic evaluation of healthcare.

> Briggs A, Claxton K, Sculpher M. *Decision Modelling for Health Economic Evaluation*. Oxford: Oxford University Press, 2006

Also look for any articles written by the International Society for Pharmacoeconomics and Outcomes Research (ISPOR). Their website has a number of resources for researchers including a series on best practices: http://www.ispor.org/research/research_index.asp. Their book on terminology is a useful resource for understanding economic evaluation concepts.

> Berger ML, Bingefors K, Hedblom EC, Pashos CL, Torrance GW, Smith MD, editors. *Health Care Cost, Quality, and Outcomes: ISPOR Book of Terms*. Lawrencevill, NJ: International Society for Pharmacoeconomics and Outcomes Research, 2003.

REFERENCES

1.   Nahin RL, Barnes PM, Stussman BJ, Bloom B. *Costs of complementary and alternative medicine (CAM) and frequency of visits to CAM practitioners: United States, 2007.* Hyattsville, MD: National Center for Health Statistics;2009.

2.   Barnes PM, Powell-Griner E, McFann K, Nahin RL. *Complementary and alternative medicine use among adults: United States, 2002.* Hyattsville, MA: National Center for Health Statistics;2004.

3.   Eisenberg DM, Davis RB, Ettner SL, et al. Trends in alternative medicine use in the United States, 1990-1997. *JAMA.* 1998;280(18):1569-1575.

4.   Eisenberg DM, Kessler RC, Foster C, Norlock FE, Calkins DR, Delbanco TL. Unconventional medicine in the United States: prevalence, costs, and patterns of use. *New Engl J Med.* 1993;328:246-252.

5.   Spinks J, Hollingsworth B. Are the economics of complementary and alternative medicine different to conventional medicine? *Expert Rev Pharmacoecon Outcomes Res.* 2009;9(1):1-4.

6.   Drummond M, Manca A, Sculpher M. Increasing the generalizability of economic evaluations: recommendations for the design, analysis, and reporting of studies. *Int J Technol Assess Health Care.* 2005;21(2):165-171.

7.   Drummond M, M. B, Cook J, et al. Transferability of economic evaluations across jurisdictions: ISPOR good research practices task force report. *Value Health.* 2009;12(4):409-418.

8.   National Center for Complementary and Alternative Medicine. What is complementary and alternative medicine (CAM)? [Website]. 2011; http://nccam.nih.gov/health/whatiscam/. Accessed October 29, 2011.

9.   Bonafede M, Dick A, Noyes K, Klein JD, Brown T. The effect of acupuncture utilization on healthcare utilization. *Med Care.* 2008;46:41-48.

10. Metz RD, Nelson CF, LaBrot T, Pelletier KR. Chiropractic care: is it substitution care or add-on care in corporate medical plans? *J Occup Environ Med.* 2004;46(8):847-855.

11. Bonsel GJ, Rutten FFH, Uyl-de Groot CA. Economic evaluation alongside cancer trials: methodological and practical aspects. *Eur J Cancer.* 1993;29A(Suppl 7):S10-S14.

12. Williams NH, Edwards RT, Linck P, et al. Cost-utility analysis of osteopathy in primary care: results from a pragmatic randomized controlled trial. *Fam Pract.* 2004;21(6):643-650.

13. Gold MR, Patrick DL, Torrance GW, et al. Identifying and valuing outcomes. In: Gold MR, Siegel JE, Russell LB, Weinstein MC, eds. *Cost-Effectiveness in Health and Medicine.* New York: Oxford University Press; 1996:82-134.

14. van den Berg I, Kaandorp GC, Bosch JL, Duvekot JJ, Arends LR, Hunink MGM. Cost-effectiveness of breech version by acupuncture-type interventions on BL 67, including moxibustion, for women with a breech foetus at 33 weeks gestation: a modelling approach. *Complement Ther Med.* 2010;18(2):67-77.

15. Hollinghurst S, Shaw A, Thompson EA. Capturing the value of complementary and alternative medicine: including patient preferences in economic evaluation. *Complement Ther Med.* 2008;16:47-51.

16. Wilson CJ, Datta SK. Tai chi for the prevention of fractures in a nursing home population: an economic analysis. *J Clin Outcomes Manage.* 2001;8(3):19-27.

17. Berger ML, Bingefors K, Hedblom EC, Pashos CL, Torrance GW, Smith MD, eds. *Health Care Cost, Quality, and Outcomes: ISPOR Book of Terms.* Lawrencevill, NJ: International Society for Pharmacoeconomics and Outcomes Research; 2003.

18. Gold MR, Siegel JE, Russell LB, Weinstein MC, eds. *Cost-Effectiveness in Health and Medicine.* New York: Oxford University Press; 1996.

19. Drummond M, O'Brien B, Economics Workgroup. Economic analysis alongside clinical trials: practical considerations. *J Rheumatol.* 1995;22(7):1418-1419.

20. Reinhold T, Witt CM, Jena S, Brinkhaus B, Willich SN. Quality of life and cost-effectiveness of acupuncture treatment in patients with osteoarthritis pain. *Eur J Health Econ.* 2008;9(3):209-219.

21.   Witt CM, Jena S, Selim D, et al. Pragmatic randomized trial evaluating the clinical and economic effectiveness of acupuncture for chronic low back pain. *Am J Epidemiol.* 2006;164(5):487-496.

22.   Witt CM, Reinhold T, Brinkhaus B, Roll S, Jena S, Willich SN. Acupuncture in patients with dysmenorrhea: a randomized study on clinical effectiveness and cost-effectiveness in usual care. *Am J Obstet Gynecol.* 2008;198(2):166.e161-161.e168.

23.   Witt CM, Reinhold T, Jena S, Brinkhaus B, Willich SN. Cost-effectiveness of acupuncture treatment in patients with headache. *Cephalalgia.* 2008;28(4):334-345.

24.   Witt CM, Reinhold T, Jena S, Brinkhaus B, Willich SN. Cost-effectiveness of acupuncture in women and men with allergic rhinitis: a randomized controlled study in usual care. *Am J Epidemiol.* 2009;169(5):562-571.

25.   Zarnke KB, Levine MAH, O'Brien BJ. Cost-benefit analyses in the health-care literature: don't judge a study by its label. *J Clin Epidemiol.* 1997;50(7):813-822.

26.   Drummond MF, Sculpher MJ, Torrance GW, O'Brien BJ, Stoddart GL. *Methods for the Economic Evaluation of Health Care Programmes.* Third ed. Oxford: Oxford University Press; 2005.

27.   Herman PM, Szczurko O, Cooley K, Mills EJ. Cost-effectiveness of naturopathic care for chronic low back pain. *Altern Ther Health Med.* Mar-Apr 2008;14(2):32-39.

28.   Brown APL, Kennedy ADM, Torgerson DJ, Campbell J, Webb JAG, Grant AM. The OMENS trial: opportunistic evaluation of musculo-skeletal physician care among orthopaedic outpatients unlikely to require surgery. *Health Bull.* 2001;59(3):199-210.

29.   Drummond MF, O'Brien B, Stoddart GL, Torrance GW. *Methods for the Economic Evaluation of Health Care Programmes.* Second ed. Oxford: Oxford University Press; 1997.

30.   Trichard M, Lamure E, Chaufferin G. Study of the practice of homeopathic general practitioners in France. *Homeopathy.* 2003;92:135-139.

31.   Busato A, Eichenberger R, Kunzi B. Extent and structure of health insurance expenditures for complementary and alternative medicine in Swiss primary care. *BMC Health Serv Res.* Oct 11 2006;6:132.

32. Ratcliffe J, Thomas KJ, MacPherson H, Brazier J. A randomised controlled trial of acupuncture care for persistent low back pain: cost effectiveness analysis. *BMJ.* 15 Sep 2006;333(7569):626.

33. Thomas KJ, MacPherson H, Thorpe I, et al. Randomised controlled trial of a short course of traditional acupuncture compared with usual care for persistent non-specific low back pain. *BMJ.* Sep 23 2006;333:623-626.

34. Hlatky MA. Economic endpoints in clinical trials. *Epidemiol Rev.* 2002;24(1):80-84.

35. Luce BR, Manning WG, Siegel JE, et al. Estimating costs in cost-effectiveness analysis. In: Gold MR, Siegel JE, Russell LB, Weinstein MC, eds. *Cost-Effectiveness in Health and Medicine.* New York: Oxford University Press; 1996.

36. Neumann PJ. Costing and perspective in published cost-effectiveness analysis. *Med Care.* July 2009;47(Suppl 1):S28-S32.

37. Garrison LP, Mansley EC, Abbott TA, Bresnahan BW, Hay JW, Smeeding J. Good research practices for measuring drug costs in cost-effectiveness analyses: a societal perspective: the ISPOR Drug Cost Task Force report—part II. *Value Health.* 2010;13(1):8-13.

38. Weinstein MC, Siegel JE, Garber AM, et al. Productivity costs, time costs and health-related quality of life: a response to the Erasmus Group. *Health Econ.* 1997;6:505-510.

39. Russell LB. Completing costs: patients' time. *Med Care.* 2009;47:S89-S93.

40. Tilling C, Krol M, Tsuchiya A, Brazier J, Brouwer W. In or out? Income losses in health state valuations: a review. *Value Health.* 2010;13(2):298-305.

41. Weinstein MC. Comment - Theoretically correct cost-effectiveness analysis. *Med Decis Making.* 1999;19(4):381-382.

42. Ramsey S, Willke R, Briggs A, et al. Good research practices for cost-effectiveness analysis alongside clinical trials: the ISPOR RCT-CEA Task Force report. *Value Health.* 2005;8(5):521-533.

43. Walworth DD. Procedural-support music therapy in the healthcare setting: a cost-effectiveness analysis. *J Pediatr Nurs.* Aug 2005;20(4):276-284.

44. Drummond M. Economic analysis alongside clinical trials: problems and potential. *J Rheumatol.* 1995;22:1403-1407.

45. Drummond MF, Davies L. Economic analysis alongside clinical trials: revisiting the methodological issues. *Int J Technol Assess Health Care.* 1991;7(4):561-573.

46. Garber AM, Weinstein MC, Torrance GW, Kamlet MS. Theoretical foundations of cost-effectiveness analysis. In: Gold MR, Siegel JE, Russell LB, Weinstein MC, eds. *Cost-Effectiveness in Health and Medicine.* New York: Oxford University Press; 1996:82-134.

47. O'Sullivan AK, Thompson D, Drummond MF. Collection of health-economic data alongside clinical trials: is there a future for piggyback evaluations? *Value Health.* 2005;8(1):67-79.

48. Doran CM, Chang DH-T, Kiat H, Bensoussan A. Review of economic methods used in complementary medicine. *J Altern Complementary Med.* 2010;16(5):591-595.

49. Tunis SR, Stryer DB, Clancy CM. Practical clinical trials: increasing the value of clinical research for decision making in clinical and health policy. *JAMA.* 2003;290(12):1624-1632.

50. Thorpe KE, Zwarenstein M, Oxman AD, et al. A pragmatic-explanatory continuum indicator summary (PRECIS): a tool to help trial designers. *J Clin Epidemiol.* 2009;62:464-475.

51. Herman PM, Sherman KJ, Erro JH, Cherkin DC, Milliman B, Adams LA. A method for describing and evaluating naturopathic whole practice. *Altern Ther Health Med.* July/Aug 2006;12(4):20-28.

52. Bond GR, Evans L, Salyers MP, et al. Measurement of fidelity in psychiatric rehabilitation. *Ment Health Serv Res.* 2000;2:75-87.

53. UK BEAM Trial Team. United Kingdom back pain exercise and manipulation (UK BEAM) randomised trial: effectiveness of physical treatments for back pain in primary care. *BMJ.* 2004:1-8.

54. UK BEAM Trial Team. United Kingdom back pain exercise and manipulation (UK BEAM) randomised trial: cost effectiveness of physical treatments for back pain in primary care. *BMJ.* 2004;329:1-7.

55. Underwood M, O'Meara S, Harvey E, UK BEAM Trial Team. The acceptability to primary care staff of a multidisciplinary training package on acute back pain guidelines. *Fam Pract.* 2002;19(5):511-515.

56.	Frost H, Klaber Moffett J, Moser JS, Fairbank JC. Randomised controlled trial for evaluation of fitness programme for patients with chronic low back pain. *BMJ*. 1995;310:151-154.

57.	Klaber Moffett J, Torgerson D, Bell-Syer S, et al. Randomised controlled trial of exercise for low back pain: clinical outcomes, costs, and preferences. *BMJ*. 1999;319:279-283.

58.	Harvey E, Burton AK, Moffett JK, Breen A. Spinal manipulation for low-back pain: a treatment package agreed by the UK chiropractic, osteopathy and physiotherapy professional associations. *Manual Ther*. 2003;8(1):46-51.

59.	Ellwein LB, Drummond MF. Economic analysis alongside clinical trials: bias in the assessment of economic outcomes. *Int J Technol Assess Health Care*. 1996;12(4):691-697.

60.	Briggs A, Claxton K, Sculpher M. *Decision Modelling for Health Economic Evaluation*. Oxford: Oxford University Press; 2006.

61.	Shadish WR, Cook TD, Campbell DT. *Experimental and Quasi-Experimental Designs for Generalized Causal Inference*. Boston: Houghton Mifflin; 2002.

62.	Benson K, Hartz AJ. A comparison of observational studies and randomized controlled trials. *New Engl J Med*. 2000;342:1878-1886.

63.	Concato J, Shah N, Horwitz RI. Randomized, controlled trials, observational studies, and the hierarchy of research designs. *New Engl J Med*. 2000;342:1887-1892.

64.	Haas M, Sharma R, Stano M. Cost-effectiveness of medical and chiropractic care for acute and chronic low back pain. *J Manipulative Physiol Ther*. 2005;28(8):555-563.

65.	Legorreta AP, Metz RD, Nelson CF, Ray S, Chernicoff HO, DiNubile NA. Comparative analysis of individuals with and without chiropractic coverage: patient characteristics, utilization, and costs. *Arch Intern Med*. 2004;164(18):1985-1992.

66.	Buxton MJ, Drummond MF, Van Hout BA, et al. Modelling in economic evaluation: an unavoidable fact of life. *Health Econ*. 1997;6:217-227.

67.	Siebert U. When should decision-analytic modeling be used in the economic evaluation of health care? *Eur J Health Econ*. 2003;4:143-150.

68.   Kim N, Yang B, Lee T, Kwon S. An economic analysis of usual care and acupuncture collaborative treatment on chronic low back pain: a Markov model decision analysis. *BMC Complement Altern Med.* 2010;10:74.

69.   Weinstein MC, O'Brien B, Hornberger J, et al. Principles of good practice for decision analytic modeling in health-care evaluations: report for the ISPOR task force on good research practices--modeling studies. *Value Health.* 2003;6(1):9-17.

70.   Polsky D, Glick H. Costing and cost analysis in randomized controlled trials: caveat emptor. *Pharmacoeconomics.* 2009;27(3):179-188.

71.   Cleary-Guida MB, Okvat HA, Oz MC, Ting W. A regional survey of health insurance coverage for complementary and alternative medicine: current status and future ramifications. *J Altern Complement Med.* 2001;7(3):269-273.

72.   Finkler SA. The distinction between cost and charges. *Ann Intern Med.* 1982;96:102-109.

73.   Pit S, Byles J. Older Australians' medication use: self-report by phone showed good agreement and accuracy compared with home visit. *J Clin Epidemiol.* 2010;63(4):428-434.

74.   Evans C, Crawford B. Patient self-reports in pharmacoeconomic studies: their use and impact on study validity. *Pharmacoeconomics.* 1999;15(3):241-256.

75.   van den Brink M, van den Hout WB, Stiggelbout AM, Putter H, van de Velde CJH, Kievit J. Self-reports of health-care utilization: diary or questionnaire? *Int J Technol Assess Health Care.* 2005;21(3):298-304.

76.   Mauskopf J, Schulman K, Bell L, Glick H. A strategy for collecting pharmacoeconomic data during phase II/III clinical trials. *Pharmacoeconomics.* 1996;9(3):264-277.

77.   Noize P, Bazin F, Dufouil C, et al. Comparison of health insurance claims and patient interviews in assessing drug use: data from the Three-City (3C) Study. *Pharmacoepidemiol Drug Safety.* 2009;18(4):310-319.

78.   Ritter PL, Stewart AL, Kaymaz H, Sobel DS, Block DA, Lorig KR. Self-reports of health care utilization compared to provider records. *J Clin Epidemiol.* 2001;54(2):136-141.

79. Goossens MEJB, Mölken MPMH, Vlaeyen JWS, van der Linden SMJP. The cost diary: a method to measure direct and indirect costs in cost-effectiveness research. *J Clin Epidemiol.* 2000;53(7):688-695.

80. Sherman EJ, Pfister DG, Ruchlin HS, et al. The collection of indirect and nonmedical direct costs (COIN) form. *Cancer.* 2001;91(4):841-853.

81. Gordon L, Scuffham P, Hayes S, Newman B. Exploring the economic impact of breast cancers during the 18 months following diagnosis. *Psycho-Oncology.* 2007;16(12):1130-1139.

82. Lund JL, Yabroff KR, Ibuka Y, et al. Inventory of data sources for estimating health care costs in the United States. *Med Care.* 2009;47(7 Suppl 1):S127-S142.

83. Dagenais S, Caro J, Haldeman S. A systematic review of low back pain cost of illness studies in the United States and internationally. *Spine J.* Jan-Feb 2008;8(1):8-20.

84. Goetzel RZ, Hawkins K, Ozminkowski RJ, Wang S. The health and productivity cost burden of the "top 10" physical and mental health conditions affecting six large U.S. employers in 1999. *J Occup Environ Med.* January 2003;45(1):5-14.

85. Maetzel A, Li L. The economic burden of low back pain: a review of studies published between 1996 and 2001. *Best Pract Res Clin Rheumatol.* 2002;16(1):23-30.

86. Johnston K, Westerfield W, Momin S, Phillippi R, Naidoo A. The direct and indirect costs of employee depression, anxiety, and emotional disorders-an employer case study. *J Occup Environ Med.* 2009;51(5):564-577.

87. Shenolikar R, Song X, Anderson JA, Chu BC, Cantrell CR. Costs of asthma among US working adults. *Am J Managed Care.* Jun 2011;17(6):409-416.

88. Hawkins K, Wang S, Rupnow MFT. Indirect cost burden of migraine in the United States. *J Occup Environ Med.* 2007;49(4):368-374.

89. Lofland JH, Pizzi L, Frick KD. A review of health-related workplace productivity loss instruments. *Pharmacoeconomics.* 2004;22(3):165-184.

90. Mattke S, Balakrishnan A, Bergamo G, Newberry SJ. A review of methods to measure health-related productivity loss. *Am J Managed Care.* 2007;13:211-217.

91. Prasad M, Wahlqvist P, Shikiar R, Shih Y-CT. A review of self-report instruments measuring health-related work productivity. *Pharmacoeconomics.* 2004;22(4):225-244.

92. Koopmanschap MA, Rutten FFH, van Ineveld BM, van Roijen L. The friction cost method for measuring indirect costs of disease. *J Health Econ.* 1995;14:171-189.

93. van den Hout WB. The value of productivity: human-capital versus friction-cost method. *Ann Rheum Dis.* 2010;69(Suppl 1):i89-i91.

94. Malone DC, Sullivan SD, Veenstra DL. Determining unit cost values for health care resources in pharmacoeconomic studies. *Formulary.* 2001;36:294-304.

95. Ramachandran A, Snehalatha C, Yamuna A, Mary S, Ping Z. Cost-effectiveness of the interventions in the primary prevention of diabetes among Asian Indians: within-trial results of the Indian Diabetes Prevention Programme (IDPP). *Diabetes Care.* Oct 2007;30(10):2548-2552.

96. Rodriguez-Roca GC, Alonso-Moreno FJ, Garcia-Jimenez A, et al. Cost effectiveness of ambulatory blood pressure monitoring in the follow-up of hypertension. *Blood Pressure.* 2006;15(1):27-36.

97. Mullins CD, Rattinger GB, Kuznik A, Koren MJ. Cost-effectiveness of intensive atorvastatin treatment in high-risk patients compared with usual care in a postgeneric statin market: economic analysis of the Aggressive Lipid-lowering Initiation Abates New Cardiac Events (ALLIANCE) study. *Clin Ther.* 2008;30(2):2204-2216.

98. Simon GE, Katon WJ, Lin EH, et al. Cost-effectiveness of systematic depression treatment among people with diabetes mellitus. *Arch Gen Psychiatry.* 2007;64(1):65-72.

99. Pavlovich WD, Waters H, Weller W, Bass EB. Systematic review of literature on the cost-effectiveness of nutrition services. *J Am Diet Assoc.* Feb 2004;104(2):226-232.

100. Boersma C, Voors AA, Visser ST, de Jong-van den Berg LT, Postma MJ. Cost effectiveness of angiotensin receptor blocker monotherapy in patients with hypertension in the Netherlands: a comparative analysis using clinical trial and drug utilization data. *Am J Cardiovasc Drugs.* 2010;10(1):49-54.

101. Bennett KJ, Torrance GW. Measuring health state preferences and utilities: rating scale, time trade-off, and standard gamble techniques. In: Spilker B, ed. *Quality of Life and Pharmoeconomics in Clinical Trials.* Second Edition ed. Philadelphia: Lippincott-Raven Publishers; 1996:253-265.

102. Sinnott PL, Joyce VR, Barnett PG. Preference Measurement in Economic Analysis Guidebook. Menlo Park CA: VA Palo Alto, Health Economics Resource Center; 2007: http://www.herc.research.va.gov/files/BOOK_419.pdf. Accessed January 27, 2012.

103. The EuroQoL Group. EuroQoL - a new facility for the measurement of health-related quality of life. *Health Policy.* 1990;16:199-208.

104. Shaw JW, Johnson JA, Coons SJ. US valuation of the EQ-5D health states: developement and testing of the D1 valuation model. *Med Care.* 2005;43:203-220.

105. Kind P, Hardman G, Macran S. *UK Population Norms for EQ-5D.* York: Centre for Health Economics, University of York; 1999.

106. Feeny D, Furlong W, Boyle M, Torrance GW. Multi-attribute health status classification systems: Health Utilities Index. *Pharmacoeconomics.* Jun 1995;7(6):490-502.

107. Brazier J, Roberts J, Deverill M. The estimation of a preference-based measure of health from the SF-36. *J Health Econ.* 2002;21:271-292.

108. Brazier JE, Roberts J. The estimation of a preference-based measure of health from the SF-12. *Med Care.* 2004;42:851-859.

109. Brazier J, Roberts J, Tsuchiya A, Busschbach J. A comparison of the EQ-5D and SF-6D across seven patient groups. *Health Econ.* 2004;13:873-884.

110. Feeny DH, Torrance GW, Furlong WJ. Health Utilities Index. In: Spilker B, ed. *Quality of Life and Pharmoeconomics in Clinical*

Trials. Second Edition ed. Philadelphia: Lippincott-Raven Publishers; 1996:239-252.

111. Luo N, Johnson JA, Shaw JW, Feeny D, Coons SJ. Self-reported health status of the general adult U.S. population as assessed by the EQ-5D and Health Utilities Index. *Med Care.* 2005;43:1078-1086.

112. Schafer T, Riehle A, Wichmann H-E, Ring J. Alternative medicine in allergies - prevalence, patterns of use, and costs. *Allergy.* 2002;57:694-700.

113. Marshall D, Bridges JFP, Hauber B, et al. Conjoint analysis applications in health - how are studies being designed and reported? An update on current practice in the published literature between 2005 and 2008. *Patient.* 2010;3(4):249-256.

114. Donaldson C, Shackley P. Does "process utility" exist? A case study of willingness to pay for laparoscopic cholecystectomy. *Soc Sci Med.* 1997;44(5):699-707.

115. Ratcliffe J, Van Haselen R, Buxton M, Hardy K, Colehan J, Partridge M. Assessing patients' preferences for characteristics associated with homeopathic and conventional treatment of asthma: a conjoint analysis study. *Thorax.* 2002;57:503-508.

116. Miller KM, Hofstetter R, Krohmer H, Zhang ZJ. How should consumers' willingness to pay be measured? An empirical comparison of state-of-the-art approaches. *J Marketing Res.* Feb 2011;48(1):172-184.

117. Mauskopf JA, Paul JE, Grant DM, Stergachis A. The role of cost-consequence analysis in healthcare decision-making. *Pharmacoeconomics.* 1998;13(3):277-288.

118. Long AF. Outcome measurement in complementary and alternative medicine: unpicking the effects. *J Altern Complement Med.* 2002;8(6):777-786.

119. O'Connol, Jonas W. [waiting for this reference]. 2003.

120. IN-CAM Outcomes Database. 2012. http://www.outcomesdatabase.org/content/framework-outcome-domains. Accessed April 12, 2012.

121. Tonelli MR, Callahan TC. Why alternative medicine cannot be evidence-based. *Acad Med.* 2001;76:1213-1220.

122. Mason S, Tovey P, Long AF. Evaluating complementary medicine: methodological challenges of randomised controlled trials. *BMJ.* 2002;325:832-834.

123. Cassidy CM. Social science theory and methods in the study of alternative and complementary medicine. *J Altern Complement Med.* 1995;2:19-40.

124. Nahin RL, Strauss SE. Research into complementary and alternative medicine: problems and potential. *BMJ.* 2001;322:161-164.

125. Gartlehner G, Hansen RA, Nissman D, Lohr KN, Carey TS. A simple and valid tool distinguished efficacy from effectiveness studies. *J Clin Epidemiol.* 2006;59:1040-1048.

126. Godwin M, Ruhland L, Casson I, et al. Pragmatic controlled clinical trials in primary care: the struggle between external and internal validity. *BMC Med Res Methodol.* 2003;3:28.

127. Little P, Lewith G, Webley F, et al. Randomised controlled trial of Alexander technique lessons, exercise, and massage (ATEAM) for chronic and recurrent back pain. *BMJ.* 2008;337:a884.

128. Braga M, Gianotti L, Vignali A, Schmid A, Nespoli L, Di Carlo V. Hospital resources consumed for surgical morbidity: effects of preoperative arginine and w-3 fatty acid supplementation on costs. *Nutrition.* 2005;21:1078-1086.

129. Hollinghurst S, Sharp D, Ballard K, et al. Randomised controlled trial of Alexander technique lessons, exercise, and massage (ATEAM) for chronic and recurrent back pain: economic evaluation. *BMJ.* 2008;337:a2656.

130. Hollis S, Campbell F. What is meant by intention to treat analysis? Survey of published randomised controlled trials. *BMJ.* 1999;319:670-674.

131. Oostenbrink JB, Al MJ, Rutten-van Molken MPMH. Methods to analyse cost data of patients who withdraw in a clinical trial setting. *Pharmacoeconomics.* 2003;21(15):1103-1112.

132. Briggs A, Clark T, Wolstenholme J, Clarke P. Missing...presumed at random: cost-analysis of incomplete data. *Health Econ.* 2003;12:377-392.

133. Manca A, Palmer S. Handling missing data in patient-level cost-effectiveness analysis alongside randomised clinical trials. *Appl Health Econ Health Policy*. 2005;4(2):65-75.

134. McKnight PE, McKnight KM, Sidani S, Figueredo AJ. *Missing Data: A Gentle Introduction*. New York: The Guilford Press; 2007.

135. Thompson SG, Barber JA. How should cost data in pragmatic randomised trials be analysed? *BMJ*. 29 Apr 2000;320:1197-1200.

136. Barber JA, Thompson SG. Analysis of cost data in randomized trials: an application of the non-parametric bootstrap. *Stat Med*. 2000;19:3219-3236.

137. Barber JA, Thompson SG. Analysis and interpretation of cost data in randomised controlled trials: review of published studies. *BMJ*. 1998;317:1195-1200.

138. Briggs AH, Wonderling DE, Mooney CZ. Pulling cost-effectiveness analysis up by its bootstraps: a non-parametric approach to confidence interval estimation. *Health Econ*. 1997;6:327-340.

139. Efron B, Tibshirani RJ. *An Introduction to the Bootstrap*. Boca Raton: Chapman & Hall/CRC; 1993.

140. Briggs A. Handling uncertainty in economic evaluation. *BMJ*. 1999;319:120.

141. Lothgren M, Zethraeus N. Definition, interpretation and calculation of cost-effectiveness acceptability curves. *Health Econ*. 2000;9:623-630.

142. Siegel JE, Weinstein MC, Torrance GW. Reporting cost-effectiveness studies and results. In: Gold MR, Siegel JE, Russell LB, Weinstein MC, eds. *Cost-Effectiveness in Health and Medicine*. New York: Oxford University Press; 1996.

143. Gerkens S, Crott R, Cleemput I, et al. Comparison of three instruments assessing the quality of economic evaluations: a practical exercise on economic evaluations of the surgical treatment of obesity. *Int J Technol Assess Health Care*. 2008;24(3):318-325.

144. Siegel JE, Weinstein MC, Russell LB, Gold MR. Recommendations for reporting cost-effectiveness analyses. *JAMA*. 1996;276(16):1339-1341.

145.   Ofman JJ, Sullivan SD, Neumann PJ, et al. Examining the value and quality of health economic analyses: implications of utilizing the QHES. *J Managed Care Pharm.* 2003;9(1):53-61.

146.   Ramsey SD, Sullivan SD. Weighing the economic evidence: guidelines for critical assessment of cost-effectiveness analyses. *J Am Board Fam Pract.* 1999;12(6):477-485.

147.   Drummond MF, Jefferson TO, BMJ Economic Evaluation Working Party. Guidelines for authors and peer reviewers of economic submissions to the BMJ. *BMJ.* August 3 1996;313:275-283.

148.   Wonderling D, Vickers AJ, Grieve R, McCarney R. Cost effectiveness analysis of a randomised trial of acupuncture for chronic headache in primary care. *BMJ.* 2004;328(7442):747.

149.   Donaldson C, Currie G, Mitton C. Cost effectiveness analysis in health care: contraindications. *BMJ.* 2002;325(7369):891-894.

150.   Sculpher MJ, Pang FS, Manca A, et al. Generalisability in economic evaluation studies in healthcare: a review and case studies. *Health Technol Assess.* 2004;8(49).

INDEX

medical chart, 5, 32, 39, **40-41**

medical records, 38, 39, **40-41**

micro-costing, 37, 48

missing data, **62-63**

modeling studies, 40, 43, 66

modeling, 4, 5, 27, 32, **35-36**, 39, 40, 43, 57, 60, 66, 69, 71

observational data/studies, 5, 27, **32-34**, 38, 39, 40, 41, 43, 56, 57

opportunity cost, 6, **21-22**, 24, 46, 47

patient perspective, 2, 13, 14, 23, 24, 40, 44, 45, 50

payer perspective, 13, 20, 22, 40

perspective, 2, **13-14**, 16, 17, 18, 20, 21, **22-24**, 37, 40, 41, 44, 45, 47, 50, 52, 53, 59, 61, 62, 69

piggyback economic evaluation, 28

preference weights, 15, 16, 24, 49, 50, 51

presenteeism, 45, 46, 55

productivity losses/costs, 1, 20, 21, 23, 24, **45-46**, 51, 53, 66

published data/sources, 37, **43-45**, 47

quality-adjusted life-years (QALYs), **3**, 12, 14, 15, 16, 17, 21, 24, 36, 50, 51, 54, 53, 58, 64, 65

resource use, 6, **21**, 25, 31, 32, 34, 37, 38, 40, 41, 42, 43, 47

sample size, 28, **31**, 33

sensitivity analysis, 26, 38, 46, 48, 62, 63, **65-66**

societal perspective, **13-14**, 16, 20, 21, 23, 24, 40, 41, 44, 45, 47, 50, 52, 54, 58, 61, 62, 69

study duration, 28, **31-32**, 33

transferability, 4, 30, 40, 47, 69

treatment fidelity, 3, 29, 30, 31

unit cost/price, 6, 11, 21, 34, 37, 40, **47-48**, 61, 65, 66, 69

utility(ies), 15, 16, 36, 49, 50, 51, 53

www.ingramcontent.com/pod-product-compliance
Lightning Source LLC
Chambersburg PA
CBHW050548280326
41933CB00011B/1771